SANDINISTA ECONOMICS IN PRACTICE

SANDINISTA ECONOMICS IN PRACTICE

An Insider's Critical Reflections

by
Alejandro Martínez Cuenca

Prologue by Sergio Ramírez
Foreword by Roberto Pizarro

With a Chronology by
María Rosa Renzi and
Alejandro Martínez Cuenca

South End Press   Boston

Translation: Nick Cooke, Hamlet Translations
Cover design: Chuck Aliberti
English edition edited and produced by the South End Press collective
Manufactured in the U.S.A.
Originally published in Spanish by Editorial Nueva Nicaragua (1990) under the title "Nicaragua: Una década de desafíos"

Library of Congress Cataloging-in-Publication Data
Martínez Cuenca, Alejandro, 1947-
[Nicaragua, una década de desafíos. English]
Sandinista economics in practice: an insider's critical reflections / a dialogue between Alejandro Martínez Cuenca and Roberto Pizarro; prologue by Sergio Ramírez ; with a chronology by María Rosa Renzi and Alejandro Martínez Cuenca; [translation, Nick Cooke].
    p.   cm.
Translation of: Nicaragua, una década de desafíos.
ISBN 0-89608-431-0 (paper)
ISBN 0-89608-432-9 (cloth)
1. Martínez Cuenca, Alejandro, 1947-   —Interviews.
2. Nicaragua—Politics and government—1979-   3. Nicaragua—Politics and government—1979- —Chronology. 4. Economists—Nicaragua-Interviews. 5. Cabinet officers—Nicaragua—Interviews.
I. Pizarro, Robert. II. Renzi, María Rosa. III. Title.
F1528.22.M35A3   1992
972.8505'3—dc20   91-33110
                                          CIP

South End Press, 116 St. Botolph Street, Boston, MA 02115
99 98 97 96 95 94 93 92   1 2 3 4 5 6 7 8

Contents

Acknowledgments

With the deepest respect, I first acknowledge the thousands of men and women who gave their lives during this decade of struggle for self-determination and the transformation of our society. I thank the Sandinista Front for National Liberation for the opportunity it gave me to be a part of this history.

I thank all those *compañeros* and *compañeras* who read the manuscript with interest and who contributed to its enrichment. In particular, I would like to make note of the tireless work carried out by Roberto Pizarro and María Rosa Renzi who dedicated countless hours to the work of ordering and designing the dialogue from which this book originated. I am deeply grateful to them and to the Swedish Development Agency (SIDA) for their financial support in the translation of this book. Thanks also to the South End Press collective, and to my editor Karin Aguilar-San Juan, for their commitment to this project and to our Nicaraguan struggle.

I also thank my wife Claudia, my daughter Claudia Agustina, and my sons Alejandro Ernesto and Juan Ignacio, who gave me strength and encouragement in the face of adversity.

—Alejandro Martínez Cuenca

Translator's note

In the English translation of this book, Spanish terms such as *compañero* appear in italics except for the words "Comandante" and "campesino." The first has come into common usage in the English language, largely as a result of 11 years of news reports about the Nicaraguan revolution, and the second is a more apt word than the alternatives offered by literal translations such as peasant (more appropriate for 19th century Europe) or farmer (more appropriate for a country like the United States).

All acronyms, when they refer to Latin American organizations or entities, are given in their Spanish form. So, for example, the acronym for the Sandinista Front for National Liberation is FSLN, and not SFNL.

—Nick Cooke

Prologue by Sergio Ramírez

Looking at the ten years of Sandinista government, during the multiple challenges we faced, what stands out in front of everything else are the unprecedented, and many times contradictory, experiences we confronted in this period. It is simply not possible to set out a methodological examination that takes a theoretical model as a reference point, and then draw conclusions about the successes and failures of our revolution. The reason is that no model ever existed as such. This is most clear when we talk about the economy.

The Sandinista revolution was born in the midst of dreams for change that reality was remolding with painful blows, frustrating many of these dreams, leaving others unfinished along the road. Yet some dreams really were possible to achieve despite the constant siege to which we were subjected.

The transformation of the basic characteristics of the social and economic structure of the country was possible; defense and the consolidation of sovereignty and national identity was possible; and giving the country a real democracy for the first time in our history was possible. And all that was done in the midst of a war of aggression which—because of its unprecedented proportions in terms of death and destruction, the economic blockade, and the financial boycott—did not allow us to sustain economic growth.

To lead and organize an economy in wartime is an experience few people have had. Many of us graduated as economists in the best "school" possible, real life, where we faced the daily challenge of changing problems. We had to face up to those problems with dedication, without timetables, in interminable discussions, and assume shared responsibility.

This difficult process of managing a revolutionary economy is what Dr. Alejandro Martínez Cuenca, a leading member of the Sandinista government's economic team, focuses on from the perspective of his personal experience. His retrospective is badly needed now, when we need to learn the lessons of our experience so we will be able to look to the future of the revolution, the continuity of which we are obliged to guarantee with a critical vision. Above all, by the time we return to government as a party, we should have learned from our mistakes and assessed the value of our skills.

Thoughtful contributions like this are needed in order to create an overall appreciation of our work during this period, and to open up an ongoing critical discussion about the role we fulfilled as men and women given over to the popular cause. This cause continues to live in us as it did on the first day when we assumed forever our commitment to the revolution.

—Sergio Ramírez

former Vice-president of Nicaragua

Foreword by Roberto Pizarro

I was in exile in England from my native Chile when I first heard the Indian names Masaya, Monimbó, Matagalpa, and Estelí. From the last half of 1978 until July 1979, one could read in the British press that the people of those Nicaraguan cities and other hidden places in that country in the middle of the Central American isthmus were rising up against Latin America's longest-standing dynasty.

Fate led me from my cold and rainy isolation to Nicaragua in October. An Uruguayan friend phoned me in the small city of Uckfield to ask me to collaborate on a course in international trade for officials of the new Ministry of Foreign Trade in 3Nicaragua.

The mission was to have lasted 15 days, yet I stayed a month. Alongside my work, I interviewed children and youth who had participated directly in the insurrection, housewives who had given shelter to combatants, Christians in base-level communities who had taught the Gospel as a weapon of rebellion against the dictatorship, businesspeople who had sought to free themselves from the economic yoke of Somoza, and Latin American revolutionaries who had participated in decisive military battles which, when the Sandinista triumph came, encouraged their hopes for defeating the other dictatorships of the Southern Cone (Chile and Argentina).

At this time, I met the Minister of Foreign Trade, Alejandro Martínez Cuenca. He was not a guerrilla. He was an executive, a modern politician who attended rapidly to the telephone and who signed papers with a sureness, as though there were no doubts that what was being done was being done well. Right away, he assailed me with questions about the theme of my mission, about the comparative advantages of nineteenth-century economist David Ricardo, about the theory of unequal exchange, and about the economic thought of the CEPAL (Economic Commission for Latin America). After I passed this unique test, the minister asked me about the Chilean experience and the comparisons I would make to the Nicaraguan economic transition.

That first conversation was unusually long, prompting an unexpected question: "Are you interested in working in Nicaragua?" I didn't think about it for even a minute before responding affirmatively.

I returned to Nicaragua at the end of July 1981 and worked as an advisor to Martínez Cuenca for nine years: first in the Ministry of Foreign Trade and, from December 1988 on, in the Planning Ministry.

The defeat of my people and of the people of Argentina (where I spent my first exile) made me feel that Nicaragua's struggles were mine, too: the taking of the National Palace, the flight of Somoza, and the Sandinista triumph were events with which I identified wholeheartedly. To work in Nicaragua was to recover the identity my people lost in British territory. Later, I would find myself with Chileans along the tree-lined avenues of teeming Santiago and listen to the drums of the throngs of the poor protesting poverty in Argentina's May Plaza.

The way I see it, the Sandinista Peoples' Revolution did not merely seal the fate of a 40-year dynasty. It stood as an extraordinary phenomenon for the peoples of Central and Latin America. After the failures of the national peoples' revolutions that were attempted in Latin America at the end of the Sixties and the beginning of the Seventies, including the overthrow of Allende's socialism in Chile, the Sandinistas brought a ray of hope to a region crushed by opprobrious military dictatorships which not only made the poorest even poorer, but which also cast their houses into mourning with repression and death.

This revolution was born while the industrialized world was breaking with Keynesian traditions and the idea of the benevolent State. The triumphs of Margaret Thatcher in Great Britain in mid-1979 and Ronald Reagan in the United States in 1980 began a period of capitalist restructuring. The new forms that capitalist development adopted in the industrialized centers, together with the anti-people offensive unleashed on a world level, without a doubt made for a not-very-propitious framework for the materialization of the Sandinista strategy.

Nor were the political winds blowing in favor of socialism. At the end of the Seventies and the beginning of the Eighties, actually existing socialism began to break apart and lose legitimacy, especially with the development of workers' struggles in Poland, the invasion of Afghanistan by the USSR, and the war between Vietnam and Cambodia. Throughout the Eighties, the generalized disaster suffered in the economic, political, and ideological fields in what was called the socialist camp narrowed the limits of negotiation for a Nicaragua that was implementing a policy of diversified political and economic insertion into the international arena.

In the Eighties, the productive, technological, and financial restructuring of the industrialized world hit the developing world as sharply as in the Thirties. The breakdown of world trade and protectionism, combined with the multiplying of the debt, left Latin America—and Central America in particular—bankrupt. The road to development and the Sandinistas' demands for a Latin Americanist relation of nations not only encountered political obstacles, but ran contrary to the economic nature of the region itself.

Our revolutionary passion for economic and social transformation, together with the long-sought-after recovery of national dignity—the legacy of General Sandino—was faced then with a very complex reality. We faced this new economic and political situation in Latin America and the world. We needed to grapple with material, social, and ideological realities that would face us in our pursuit of the Sandinista project. The limited development of the productive forces of this agricultural country marked by a backward industrial plant, high levels of illiteracy, and a weak social infrastructure, demanded that the new Sandinista government put into play a strategy of transformation and economic recovery with a high social content. The historical demands of the urban and rural poor obliged the Sandinista government to make urgent responses in the social and economic fields.

This strategy of transformation and economic recovery is reviewed critically by Martínez Cuenca, who lays bare here the successes as well as the errors in its implementation. He also describes the institutional feudalism, and the different ideological divisions that were at play in the government. The former minister tries not only to draw a "balance sheet" over the ten-year period of Sandinista rule, but also points out possible routes into the future, so that *Sandinismo* can get into step with the new times that are passing in the world.

State-run and market-oriented economies, centralization and the formation of economic policy, the joining together of the economic and the political facets of society, and the responsibilities of the government are all discussed openly and frankly.

Particular attention is paid to the weight which was given to defense and foreign policy by the government, the Sandinista Front, and the social organizations which relegated concerns about economic themes to a secondary plane, an oversight rectified only in 1988 with the adjustment program, after the first Central American presidential summit meeting was held, resulting in what became known as the Esquipulas Accords.

The results of opinion polls—or the interpretations of them—together with the self-confidence of the Sandinista leadership made everybody lose sight of potential problems. The wearing down of the country because of the war, the economic breakdown, and the errors committed in ten years of governing finally defeated the Sandinista Front in the elections held on February 25, 1990. The electoral results were a complete surprise internationally, to the Sandinistas, and to the triumphant political coalition itself.

The cleanliness of the elections, held under the unprecedented observation of international bodies, and the peaceful transfer of power on April 25, 1990 to the new president, Violeta Chamorro, attracted the world's attention, put the leaders of the United States off balance, and shocked the orthodox left. Having been shaken up and down by severe aggression, *Sandinismo* is once again being put to the test.

The institutions created by the revolution—such as an army and a police force that are not meant to accomodate the priorities of U.S. geopolitics—present a big challenge to the new Chamorro government, to the powerful Sandinista opposition, and to U.S. policy makers. The question is whether these entities will be able to respect democracy and the new institutions that are a legacy of the Sandinistas in order to make the country viable, or will they wipe all that out and move into complete social chaos.

The agreements between the Sandinistas and the National Opposition Union (UNO) government regarding the transition signed on March 27, 1990 were a sign of political respect for the new regime. On the other hand, however, social and political tensions sharpened within less than 100 days of Chamorro's government. Two public-sector strikes rocked the country. Ultra-rightist politicians inside and outside of the government are exerting pressure to wipe out the Sandinista past, while sectors inside the FSLN are demanding a radical confrontation with the new government.

The intention of this book is to reflect about the recent past and to discuss a present loaded with tensions and probable alternatives for the uncertain paths of the future. Alejandro Martínez played an outstanding role, as much in criticizing the policy of economic centralism practiced by *Sandinismo* in the first years, as in the conception and the implementation of a new economic policy, characterizing the government's actions since the 1988 stabilization and adjustment program. In addition, as the Minister of Foreign Trade, he participated in decisive meetings confronting the financial and trade embargo imposed by the United States.

The conversations that took place between Martínez Cuenca—an important protagonist in this history—and me cover themes of crucial importance for Nicaragua: the program and structure of the Government of National Reconstruction, economic policy and its administration, foreign policy and the U.S. blockade, and the political achievements of *Sandinismo* and its prospects for the future.

In organizing the transcripts of these conversations, I give special thanks to María Rosa Renzi for her contribution, without which the elaboration of this work would have been extremely difficult. It was thanks to her persistent capacity for work and her unyielding commitment to the Nicaraguan revolution that we managed to generate out of the long dialogue sessions the basic material for this book.

Only love for Nicaragua and its people have inspired this work. Nine years of vital experience closes a chapter of my life during which the successes, failures, fears, and happiness shared with my Nicaraguan brothers and sisters stamp indelible commitments into me which will never be erased with my return to Chile, my homeland.

—Roberto Pizarro

Introduction

Twenty-eight years have transpired since I consciously made the decision to fight without rest alongside the people in order to find a way to transform the society into which I was born. I have done it with a strictly Christian, Sandinista, and deeply human conviction, making all the errors and having all the successes that come along with that.

In getting involved in the task of narrating my personal experiences in the historical epoch of ten years of the Sandinista Peoples' Revolution, I do it from a perspective of deep reflection in order to discern the routes that the future is imposing on our lives.

I agreed to write this book because I feel that a willingness to be truly self-critical will allow for new light to be shed on the Nicaraguan revolution, particularly now after the electoral defeat when we have proposed a review in order to decide the future of our party, the FSLN.

This book is in the form of a dialogue because we think it a less heavy way to raise themes which are usually loaded with a lot of technical terms. I try to develop this account of my experiences from the economic and political perspective that it fell on me to live through.

Certainly the pages of this book do not cover everything that happened, only those parts of the history in which in one way or another I was involved. Nor will the reader find the totality of my experiences, for that would have meant a much more complicated and extensive task than that which is attempted on this occasion.

I start from the fact of the indisputable achievements that the Sandinista Peoples' Revolution attained in the Eighties. The Sandinistas, the Nicaraguan people, as well as the international community must acknowledge the valuable contribution that the Sandinista Peoples' Revolution made in these ten years. For my part, I am convinced that the transformations of Nicaraguan society have been transcendental and that the sacrifice, pain, and death of thousands of men and women throughout this period have not been in vain.

We have built a Nicaragua which today enjoys democracy. With the revolution, the people won their sovereignty, their independence, and they have exercised their eminently revolutionary right to self-determination.

Nicaragua's people today enjoy fully the right to political organization and participation. There are thousands of social organizations, including 873 labor unions with a total of more than 326,000 members, and 21 political parties of varied ideological tendencies functioning in the country. Two free and honest elections have been held and are considered internationally as an example of purity in suffrage.

Throughout these ten years of the Sandinista revolution, many important gains were made in the organization of the people, gains which have been fundamental for the social advancement of women, youth, and ethnic groups, as well as for the expansion of religious activity in our country. We managed to begin to build a social democracy expressed in the distribution of social services, which in its turn constitutes a mechanism for the redistribution of income in favor of the poorest.

We built a state of law with the possibility of changes in power and with armed forces and police that respect the people's will and the political sovereignty of the Republic, a country with a political constitution where laws govern the national life and justice is administered according to the law. Today there is a Nicaragua in which four State powers—executive, legislative, judicial, and electoral—serve to preserve the constitutional order of independence and integrity.

A non-aligned and independent foreign policy was forged which upholds international law and which has played an important role in creating a new international economic order in the GATT (General Agreement on Tariffs and Trade), the SELA (Economic System of Latin America), and other economic forums. That policy has put a priority on peace and the peaceful resolution of conflicts through the United Nations, the Organization of American States, the Non-Aligned Movement, Contadora, Esquipulas, etc.

We have built a Nicaragua with a foreign policy based on international law. We brought the successful suit against the U.S. aggression towards Nicaragua to the International Court of Justice at the Hague, where the aggression was condemned, and it was ruled that the United States must compensate this country for damages and injuries suffered adding up to more than $17 billion.

These are undeniable, and some are irreversible, but the apologetic defense of all that was done does not contribute to discerning routes to the future, and so it is necessary to highlight not only the successes but also the limitations and obstacles that we had to confront and that led us to make mistakes. Although many difficulties and mistakes were made in carrying out these tasks, it has probably been in the economic field where the greatest difficulties have been found in this period.

It is in the area of the economy where the greatest problems were presented because of Nicaragua's historical backwardness, an unjust international economic order, and the consequences of the dictatorial power of Somoza, who favored external dependence and the concentration of wealth among a few. This, together with the out and out U.S. war of aggression, limited the possibilities for greater economic and social development in these last ten years.

The above explains, in large part, the economic limitations we faced, but I also think that it is necessary to make a self-critical analysis of our own errors in order to extract instructive conclusions as a party and as a nation. The central thesis of this book is that the origins of the February 1990 electoral defeat of *Sandinismo* are found many years before that election. We failed to give sufficient importance to the wearing down of the economy—not only a product of the war. The conceptual differences around centralism versus a market economy took too long to be cleared up inside of *Sandinismo*. That failure to clear up this dilemma on time led to losing valuable time at very crucial moments when Nicaragua was becoming integrated into the world market.

With this in view, I accepted the challenge of this book, conscious that these are personal judgments and, therefore, subject to the margin of interpretation of each one's experience. I hope they will contribute to the spirit of historical review that present-day reality imposes on us.

—Alejandro Martínez Cuenca

The Electoral Defeat of *Sandinismo*

° *Why did the Sandinista Front lose the February 25, 1990 elections?*

Nicaragua was worn down considerably as a result of the war, and in addition we must acknowledge the consequences of our own mistakes. The war was devastating for Nicaraguan society: We went into the elections under very difficult conditions. The economic adjustment program which we began to implement in early 1988 had still not assured that recovery was on the horizon, and the population was tired of so much sacrifice.

We lost the elections as a result of a very rational vote by the Nicaraguan people. It was a vote cast against war and *for* peace. I'm not so sure that it was a vote to reject the FSLN, although it could be that there were voters who categorically rejected the presence of the FSLN in power. Violeta Chamorro[1] won because, for many, it was clear that she had a greater chance of closing that chapter of the war.

The U.S. strategy was effective in selling the notion that a victory by President Chamorro would mean the end of the war, while our public discourse gave no signs that, in the short term, normal relations would be renewed with the United States nor would armed conflict end. The people voted for peace, for an end to the sacrifices and sufferings that they had had to go through during the period of severe aggression. It was a conscious vote by people who did not see the ability in the FSLN to assure them the good life and the peace that they longed for.

° *Inside the government and the FSLN National Directorate, was the possibility of losing ever considered?*

Frankly, no.

° *How can such isolation from reality be explained? Was it because of FSLN self-sufficiency, an incapacity for objective analysis, or did the people of Nicaragua turn about-face at the very end of the election campaign?*

Defeat was not considered because we were highly ideologized; we were convinced that the people couldn't vote against their own class interests. We didn't give enough importance to the serious situation of survival in the countryside and to the deep contradictions that the war had introduced among mothers, youth, and fathers. We lost sight of the drama of the war and its psychological and human effects.

The FSLN slogan "Everything will be better" did not hold up in practice since in the eyes of the majority of the people this meant stopping the war, and the people didn't see clear signs that the FSLN could make that a reality. Even our own political discourse was not in harmony with that slogan; it was overly charged with anti-U.S. rhetoric. We overestimated ourselves by thinking that the people saw their interests only in us.

This error in appraising the people's feelings was, in a way, a continuation of the bad habit of conceiving of the party as centralized, extremely disciplined, verticalist or top-down, and charged with a great deal of voluntarism. In such conditions, party behavior was extrapolated to the rest of society. That was a serious mistake since society behaves with rules different from the strict discipline that a political party can impose.

° *How do you explain that the election polls carried out during the campaign were so different from the final results?*

The poll results themselves were not mistaken; in fact, throughout the whole election campaign, they consistently showed that the FSLN was not doing well. The problem was that there were too many "undecided" voters and the mistake was to try to extrapolate conclusions about the way that this large segment would vote as is done normally with opinion polls in other countries. The election results showed this to be a tremendous mistake.

The government of President Violeta Chamorro

° *Nicaragua now has a new government. How would you assess the forces within it?*

The new government has a very weak base; it is a very heterogeneous mix of forces. The origin of its weakness lies in the fact that the forces which make it up never thought they would win the elections. Just as we overestimated ourselves, they underestimated themselves. The parties of the National Opposition Union (UNO)[2] thought that an FSLN defeat was highly unlikely, and so its election program picked up a substantial amount of political demagogy.

A faithful reflection of its demagogy was the economic program that they presented to the voters. In reality, the UNO government's economic program arose from propagandistic promises, making commitments that couldn't be fulfilled in practice. And so with a program that proposed to meet the people's demands, once in government, UNO found itself faced with strong contradictions and subject to the influence of those who would like to see the revolutionary changes introduced during the Sandinista era reversed. There was not very much room for the people's demands. A big space opened up between what was said in public and the class-biased practice of the government.

The economic program put forward by the Central Bank president, Dr. Francisco Mayorga,[3] for the first six months of President Chamorro's governmenthad unrealistic intentions of simultaneous adjustment and reactivation. This proved to be unrealistic given the present conditions of the Nicaraguan economy.

Mayorga said he would eliminate inflation in 100 days. This proved impossible to achieve, and to the contrary, during the first six months of the new government, the economy suffered a dramatic acceleration of hyperinflationary tendencies. It reached an unprecedented average monthly inflation rate of 89 percent for the first six months.

In short, since they never thought they were going to govern, UNO promised many things, and harsh reality turned its back on such offerings. Now, when governing is not just saying but doing, they point to us, to the former government, as responsible for their program's lack of viability and for their inability to keep their election promises.

As has been seen already, desperation gives rise to the arrogant attitudes which characterize some current government officials. In such conditions, when the over-ideologized ones want to implement a new project of reactivation and development, they think they can ignore the fact that there have been ten years of revolution and that a new understanding of democracy has been created in the country.

Notwithstanding, the new government also has realistic and pragmatic people in it who are looking along the route of negotiation and understanding for a solution to the country's problems.

°   *In looking at the first year of the new government, we must recognize that the strike activity that developed in the country in the first three months made it difficult to implement their program. Two massive public-sector strikes, one of them taking on a semi-insurrectional character, made it very difficult to govern.*

   The government blamed the Sandinista Party for this activity. Was that the case?

It is completely untrue that the Sandinista Front deliberately wanted to block the efforts of the new government. That would have been an enormous political error. The attitude of making the country ungovernable is not one that is held by the Sandinista Front leadership, although in the membership, some individuals still may not have accepted that we lost and that it's necessary to comprise a civic opposition in order to regain power within the framework established by the Constitution.

The labor strikes in the first months of the new regime happened because the government did not show clear signs of respect for the Constitution. I'm not going to enter into an analysis of the convenience or inconvenience of one or another strike, or whether it was opportune or not, but it's clear that such activities were not the result of a preconceived attitude assumed by *Sandinismo*. Rather, they were the product of serious errors made by the government in enacting legislation clearly in contradiction to the Constitution.

Groups on the extreme right, both inside and outside the government, also have to understand once and for all that there wasn't a military defeat here which did away with *Sandinismo*. There was a democratic transfer of government on the basis of elections within the framework of the political infrastructure created in the country over the last ten years.

The basic game rules are written down in the Constitution, and if they aren't respected, social instability and violent reactions will result. If, for example, there are campesinos who benefitted from the agrarian reform programs and some former landowners want to use the government to take away their lands, it can't be expected that those campesinos will adopt a submissive attitude.

° *An extraordinary case has been presented in Nicaragua with the change in government. Unlike any other country in Latin America, the army was born in the insurrection and organized and consolidated itself during the years of revolutionary government. The police have similar characteristics.*

We have an army and a police force that do not fit into the ideological and geopolitical patterns set by the United States. For the right, nationally and internationally, this army and this police are anomalies that have to be removed. For others, however, the army and police are two cornerstones of the new infrastructure and cannot be changed. Are the army and police stabilizing factors for the country?

For any government that wants to work within the framework of the Constitution, the guarantee of social stability is to be found in having a policy of *concertación,* in other words, having all social and economic sectors commit themselves to work together for the good of the nation through open and crystal clear negotiations. *Concertación* depends on respecting the armed forces and the police.

This army and these police are a threat only to those who don't want to recognize the existence of the revolution and the changes that have affected the country since July 19, 1979. These new, armed institutions are a threat only to those with extremist positions who want to return to the past of rule by elites.

° *The process of transition from the Sandinista to the UNO government was very fluid. The transition protocol that was signed was recognized nationally and internationally as a success. However, in the handing over of the government, the same success didn't happen in every area.*

In the area of the economy, the transition was not fluid and the country paid a high price for the paralyzing economic measures that were implemented between February 25 and April 25. To what do you attribute this?

The area of the economy was one of the most polemical in our government. It's easier to hand over the Ministry of Health and the hospitals with their programs, inventories, and budgets. But when you enter into the realm of economic policy, knowledge and control is very personalized, so a smooth transition from one government to the next is made much more difficult.

The arrogance of some new government authorities who were on the economic commission of transition made the country pay a high price. I'm not free from all blame. Maybe there were confrontational attitudes on both sides. On the one hand, there was our attitude of wanting to leave a very clear record, and on the other, there was the attitude of the representatives of the new government who didn't want this record to appear.

The fact that prior to February 25, Mayorga never thought he would become the Minister-President of the Central Bank played an important role. And when this big responsibility was thrust upon him, he became defensive, looking for scapegoats to blame when his proposed policies did not work as he had argued rhetorically during the campaign. That's why, once he assumed the post, Mayorga's discourse became considerably politicized.

° *I understand that a joint effort was made by the Sandinista government, together with some people in the incoming government and with the support of the United Nations Development Program,[4] to present a joint proposal at the second Conference of Donors in Rome in June 1990. Why was there pressure to work together?*

I would stress that the February 25 election results did not mean that there had been a revolution within the revolution. And therefore, we all—but mainly the incoming government—had the responsibility to assure that there is stability, economic recovery, and peace. For the benefit of the whole country, we felt responsible for making sure that Nicaragua would receive new outside aid.

Conscious that the international community had given an important amount of support to the economic program that we had been implementing, we felt we had the moral authority to demand even greater international co-responsibility. Moreover, it seemed that it would be useful to pass on the experience we had in economic management to the new authorities.

In short, we adopted a responsible attitude towards the country, which unfortunately did not find an adequate interlocutor in the new leadership on economic policy.

° *In spite of that attitude, when former Vice-president Sergio Ramirez,[5] went to the second Conference of Donors in*

Rome, his action provoked criticism from some Sandinistas. How do you explain the presence of Ramírez at that conference?

There were two reasons for his trip. The first Conference of Donors in Stockholm[6] was the fruit of Sandinista efforts. Second, the international community had asked at the first conference for participation by the opposition. So we felt our participation would be useful for the country since it would be looked on favorably by the international community of donors and it would help bring in more resources for the national economy. Besides, this had been contemplated in the spirit and letter of the Transition Accords.[7]

This is one proof that the Sandinistas are not in favor of placing obstacles in the way of the new government. Another is the effort made in September 1990 by former President Daniel Ortega which resulted in the commitment by the West German government to renew the aid package that had been suspended earlier.

° *You were the main promotor and protagonist in the first Conference of Donors in Stockholm. The results there, according to Mayorga, were far below the success that he later had in obtaining $180 million at the second meeting of donor countries. What is your opinion?*

In the first place, I don't believe that the results of the Stockholm meeting were as weak as people have made them out to be. It should be remembered that the success at Stockholm was not just the $40 million that was obtained in liquid foreign exchange, but also includes the political results in the context of the strong pressures placed on the participating countries by the U.S. government, and in particular, by Secretary of State James Baker.

° *Could you be more concrete?*

Baker tried unsuccessfully to pressure the Spanish, French, and Swedish governments so that they would come out in total disagreement with the holding of the first Conference of Donors in May 1989.

That conference has to be seen as a political victory for the people of Nicaragua, for the donor countries themselves, and particularly for the Swedish government, which exercised its right to support Nicaragua with autonomy. It was, at the same time, an act of reproach towards the policy pushed by the United States before the conference. From that point of view, the support that Nicaragua received was without equal, and it was something which should not be measured only in quantitative terms.

The formation of a monitoring commission directed by U.S. professor Albert Fishlow[8] was also a success. Quarterly reports were produced, which we sent to all the countries that participated in the Stockholm conference, thereby responding to the interest the international community had in following what we were doing. The program we were promoting was applauded, even by the International Monetary Fund and the Interamerican Development Bank.

So Stockholm was a success from a political perspective and also in terms of making Nicaragua's efforts known. It was that success that allowed for the holding of the second conference in Rome. That meeting was organized by the Sandinista government and was scheduled to occur before the elections. Once again, the United States forced the postponement of the conference. The second conference, held after the February 25 elections, had an attendance very similar to the first with the addition of three countries: Japan, the United States, and Great Britain. They had refused to participate in the first round, and but did agree to join in the second.

The aid that the United States said it was going to provide to the new government paved the way for other countries so that they could give without fear of reprisal. The results of the second conference were not that different from those of the first in the fresh resources obtained if you take into account that there still exist unfulfilled commitments that had been made in Stockholm.

Therefore, without underrating the results, I consider the conference in Rome to have been a joint effort of the Sandinista Front and the new government. The participation of former Vice-president Ramírez is symbolic of the positive attitude that the FSLN had with respect to the Conference of Donors. For the same reason, the FSLN also sent a delegation to the third round held in Paris in December 1990.

°   *Besides the theme of adjustment and stabilization and the resources needed for that, an impression is given that the new government places a great deal of confidence in direct foreign investment, in particular from the United States as well as from Nicaraguan exiles in Miami. What is your opinion?*

Foreign investment is very important, but it's not going to come overnight. Nor do I think that the resources that the Nicaraguans abroad have would be enough to be able to predict a substantial upswing of investment. Foreign investors are cautious. Before making bold decisions, they want to see political stability in the government, and this takes time to be tested.

° *In mid-October 1990, the government took the initiative to try to begin a process of concertación, which you mentioned earlier. What does this mean?*

Concertación in Nicaragua should not be interpreted the way it is in Europe. *Concertación* should be looked at as an attempt to find a minimum degree of convergence of objectives in order to facilitate an economic recovery within a framework of relative social and political stability.

Concertación should not be interpreted as an attempt to take the wind out of the sails of the people who have legitimate grievances when government actions interfere with their basic interests. Nor should it be interpreted as an attempt by the social forces outside the government to make a co-governing arrangement. However, it does acknowledge that in a modern democratic process, it is imperative that there be an ongoing process of mutual dialogue and feedback between those who govern and those who are governed.

° *Many people both and in and out of the country do not understand why the Sandinistas participated in concertación. Could you clarify this?*

I think it is necessary to clarify that the importance of *concertación* is found not so much in what was written down in the final document in October, but rather in what was not written but was clearly understood.

At the time of this writing, Nicaragua is about to end almost two years of rule by a new regime. Things have not been easy for anybody. On the one hand, economic performance has deteriorated dramatically, making life extremely difficult for everyone. The majority of the people have been hit by a substantial reduction in their living standard, unemployment has risen, the economic recession is affecting everybody, and there are no signs that things will change for the better in the near future. On the other hand, most of the promises made by the new government that new sources of substantial outside financing would arrive have not been fulfilled, and this has put the government in a very difficult position.

Furthermore, the majority of the people are tired of confrontation and war, and do not want to hear any more about political rivalries. The people are worried about their own economic survival and do not want to see further confrontations that can lead to a worsening of their personal economic situation.

Although this is true, it is also true that there are militant groups, both on the right and on the left, which are presently in confrontation with one another. On the one hand, we have militants on the right who would like to see the Sandinistas disappear from the political scene and who interpret the election results as being in favor of them and in favor of reverting the revolution to a position prior to 1979. On the other hand, there are those on the left who at first were on the defensive, but who were also belligerent enough to continue fighting against any attempt to dismantle the achievements of the revolution.

In addition to that, there is a lack of trust towards the government's actions. All this explains what is behind the polarization that presently exists in Nicaraguan society. There is an attitude of continuous confrontation which is making things extremely hard to handle for a heterogeneous government like the one now ruling.

Behind the forces in these militant groups on the right, one finds people like Vice-president Virgilio Godoy,[9] who is against the way the present government is made up. He is fighting for a larger share of power. In this internal struggle, he has appealed for help from Cardinal Miguel Obando y Bravo, the leadership of the business association COSEP,[10] the American embassy, and a small group of former contras who are dissatisfied about not having received the land promised them in exchange for their disarming.

The polarization between the Sandinista militants and the disaffected groups on the right has brought about the danger of a confrontation. For that reason, the agreement signed between the Sandinistas and the government during the *concertación* meetings is so important. It works to defuse confrontation, and opens up a way for the Sandinistas to play a constructive opposition role.

Concertación enables moderate elements within the government to count on a constructive opposition while defusing the risk that the groups on the extreme right would try to impose their own position in the overall economic, political, and social situation.

°   *I understand you are a close friend of President Chamorro.*
    I think it would be interesting if you could tell us a bit about

her in order to help us understand the kind of government that she leads.

I have known Violeta Chamorro for many years, thanks to the close friendship that existed between my father and her husband, Dr. Pedro Joaquín Chamorro.[11] I recall fondly the time in 1965 when I had the opportunity to show her and Pedro around London while I was studying there.

Violeta showed great strength of character in accompanying her husband to the end, going through the experiences of exile in San Carlos through to the anguish of prison and the torture that he was subjected to by the Somocista dictatorship. She also showed her firmness after the death of Dr. Chamorro. At a time prior to the insurrectional triumph, she flatly rejected the interference of the U.S. government when it was pressuring for a bigger Government Junta of National Reconstruction. That attitude, and her clandestine entrance into León on July 18, 1979, warrant a great deal of respect.

I also personally have to acknowledge the initiative she took in August 1979 in favor of the idea which I had been pushing. I wanted to set up a ministry that would help make real the project of nationalizing foreign trade and bring order to domestic commerce. I mention this in particular because at that time, there were those with opinions inside *Sandinismo* and in the Robelo[12] group which had different positions on this theme.

It seems to me that President Chamorro, despite the tremendous pressures she has been faced with, had enough energy to reaffirm the Transition Accords, in particular with respect to the High Command of the army and General Humberto Ortega.[13] This firmness is a mark that I hope, for the benefit of democracy and national sovereignty, prevails over outside pressures and over the ravings of the ultra-right.

II

The Path Towards National Reconstruction

Preparation of the Program of National Reconstruction

° *Let's go back 11 years to the time before the Sandinista insurrection and the time of the underground. It would be interesting to hear about your participation in the economic team that drafted the Program of the Government of National Reconstruction. What part did you play in that? What were your working conditions like? Who took part in drafting the program?*

The economic program of the Sandinista Front originated at the beginning of the 1970's with what was called the Historical Program. In it were defined the main outlines of what would be the new Nicaraguan society. The initiative of Carlos Fonseca[1] was decisive in this task. In the period from 1973 to 1978 my personal participation in the FSLN was more as a collaborator, providing economic information and analysis to the leadership which, in different stages, was in charge of the Sandinista Front.

In reality, the basic work of drafting the government platform began at the end of 1978 with the formation of a team that the *tercerista* faction[2] organized under the leadership of Daniel Ortega,[3] his brother Humberto, and Victor Tirado.[4] A group of *compañeros* came together in Costa Rica under the responsibility of Dr. Ernesto "Tito" Castillo[5] and Dr. Sergio Ramírez. It was "Tito" Castillo who brought me into that team, and I moved from Honduras to Costa Rica in order to dedicate myself full time to that task from the beginning of 1979 until the victory.

In Costa Rica, the team brought in Alfredo César,[6] Reynaldo Antonio Téfel,[7] Carlos Tünnermann,[8] and Dr. Roberto Mayorga.[9] Later, in order to draft the laws, Dr. Joaquin Cuadra Chamorro,[10] among others, joined. We met in an apartment-hotel in San José in the La Sabana neighborhood. We had long discussions about the content of the program and made proposals which were handed over to Daniel and Humberto Ortega.

When the outcome of the war was becoming obvious, we sped up the work of drafting the final program which was later adopted as part of the government's plan. The meetings we held were the embryo of the new government structure. Participating in them were Rogelio Ramírez,[11] Agustín Lara,[12] Alfredo César, Sergio Ramírez, "Tito" Castillo, Carlos Tünnermann, and me.

° *But you don't mention Alfonso Robelo,[13] a leading figure of the bourgeois opposition.*

Robelo didn't take part in the drafting or the discussions of the document. He took part in the discussions about the formation of the embryo of the new government where themes like nationalizing the bank and foreign trade were discussed. Robelo participated there, but in regard to the Sandinista Front's government program, the people I mentioned were the ones who took part.

° *Looking at the people who participated in drafting the document, it could be said that the economic platform is basically tercerista. Was there ever a discussion about economic strategy with the other factions of the Front?*

The concepts of a mixed economy, political pluralism, and non-alignment basically come from a broad reading of the FSLN Historic Program, and all three factions agreed on that. In effect, when we were working on the platform of government, unity of the FSLN was already at the doorstep. I can recall at least three times when, besides Daniel Ortega and Victor Tirado, Jaime Wheelock[14] and Tomás Borge[15] also participated in the discussions.

° *So there were no big conflicts or controversial areas that would have delayed discussion of the government platform?*

There were discussions around the theme of nationalizing the bank. I remember that Borge appeared one night in the Hotel Costa Rica with *compañero* René Núñez[16] and Mayorga, someone who had been completely off to the side of all the discussions about the program and platform. Mayorga had a contract as a consultant and was paid for his services to prepare some economic analyses for the Program of the Government of National Reconstruction.

At this time, Mayorga said he wasn't in complete agreement with nationalizing the bank. It had to be shown to him that the bank crisis was of such a magnitude that to not nationalize it would mean subsidizing all those owners of the bank who had been decapitalizing it. But, in general, there were no big differences.

° *You tell us about Mayorga and his different position with respect to nationalizing the bank. How do you explain then, that he appears later as one of the advisors to Comandante Henry Ruiz?*[17]

Mayorga was always very upset with the Sandinista Front, and the effort that Ruiz made to recover Mayorga is an illustration of a positive attitude of trying to attract a technician for the revolutionary project. I think that Ruiz had to go through the experience of getting to know new people, getting to know technicians, and trying to bring together some professionals. So just as he invited Mayorga, he also invited Edmundo Jarquín,[18] who, unlike Mayorga, played an important role in the revolutionary government and today is a Sandinista deputy in the National Assembly.

° *We spoke of two important elements included in the FSLN program and in the Program of the Government of National Reconstruction: nationalization of the bank and foreign trade. Agrarian reform would have to be added to this.*

What was the position of Robelo and the groups he represented before the triumph with respect to these lines of transformation which were central to the country's economic process?

I don't remember Robelo putting forward open opposition in the discussions I was involved in. Robelo, at the beginning, was even more radical than many of us. With salaries, for example, he insisted that there shouldn't be a difference greater than one to ten between the one who earned the least and the one who earned the most.

Robelo has to be attributed with the responsibility for this salary policy that resulted in a major flight of professionals in the first years of the revolutionary government for economic reasons.

Robelo's radicalism is explained to me as the typical euphoria of a capitalist who got on the train of the revolution and turns out to be more papist than the Pope. Robelo even demanded to be the one to read the decrees in public which nationalized the bank and foreign trade. But in the end, during the hard times, these people could not consistently defend the whole of the revolutionary positions.

° *What support did you receive from other Central or Latin American governments?*

We received a great deal of solidarity from the government of Costa Rica for holding our meetings within that country and for our movement in general. Rodrigo Carazo[19] helped us by facilitating our movement in Costa Rican territory. We received military support from Cuba and Panama, and material support from Venezuela. These are things which we acknowledge as being very important, although I'm not the one most qualified to judge the concrete contribution of the support received from the different governments.

° *At this technical level in which you participated, weren't there pressures or some kind of signals from the U.S. government when the implementation of a project of Somocismo without Somoza[20] was being discussed?*

First, I should make it clear that since my forced departure from Nicaragua at the end of 1978, I had been living in Honduras. I was given the responsibility by the National Directorate to serve as FSLN emissary to the Honduran governmental authorities. I also lent logistic support to the *compañeros* of the group led by Wheelock. I served as a kind of FSLN ambassador to the government of Policarpo Paz[21] and the armed forces of that country, since our activities—among them the transfer of weapons and getting some of our *compañeros* out of Honduran prisons—required contacts at the highest level.

In Costa Rica, there were emissaries from the government of the United States, in particular Ambassador William Bowdler,[22] who tried to have an influence on the triumph. Violeta Chamorro actually played an important role in standing up to these pressures. They were constant and tried to make it so that a sweeping triumph of the Front wouldn't happen and that a negotiated way out with

Somoza would be found. This was practically a daily topic of discussion in the group which was drafting the basic outlines of the economic plan.

Inauguration of the Sandinista government

° *Let's go to the first six months of the Sandinista govern-ment. What things stand out from the inauguration of the revolutionary government and the application of its eco-nomic program? Under what conditions was the govern-ment inaugurated? What surprises came out of the process of inauguration?*

In San José, I was given the job of coordinating the transfer of the new cabinet to Managua. I had to stay there the day that Comandante Humberto Ortega, "Nicho" Marenco,[23] and other *compañeros* were in a discussion with some members of the National Guard who were about to desert. By July 18, 1979 this discussion was interrupted and I was left with the responsibility of staying in a safe house in order to receive messages from Managua and send them on to the Command Post we had in Costa Rica. That's when I received one of the last calls from Managua.

By chance, the person calling was a former friend from my youth who was calling on behalf of the National Guard.[24] He was relaying the message that the Guard was willing to negotiate its surrender. At this time, the revolutionary forces were advancing on Managua and I told him there was nothing to negotiate now and that they should turn in their weapons. This for me was the clearest sign that the fall of Somoza was no longer just a dream. The next important experience was when we received the message that the *Somocistas* had tried to take away the last US$3 million that were in the Central Bank. We found that out because of a call made to us by some officials of an international bank who decided to ask us if they should proceed or not to honor a check that the Somoza regime was trying to cash at the last minute. When the Government of National Reconstruction took over, it found the Central Bank as just a building with desks and those US$3 million which we were able to save because of that telephone call.

The democratic transfer from the Sandinista government to that of President Chamorro in 1990 allowed for US$108 million in gross international reserves to be handed over to the new govern-ment. Of these, US$3 million were in the vaults of the Central Bank and US$105 million were deposited in accounts outside of the country in the bank's name. This puts the lie to the false accusation made by Mayorga, who declared that the outgoing government had not left any more reserves than what the Somocistas had left.

° *What do you remember of the first day of the Sandinista victory?*

The arrival in Managua was impressive. There were the many *compañeros* with whom we de-planed at the Managua International Airport, the installations already taken, and with the operations center of the new government in the Camino Real Hotel where instructions were received. I ended up going to the Institute of Foreign and Domestic Trade (INCEI)[25] to reorganize it.

Enthusiasm was overflowing but there was a great lack of knowledge about where to begin and how to apply the program. In July, the reduced government cabinet had already been formed, and afterwards, with the first government decrees, the new institutions were formed, and that's when new people joined in and perspectives were broadened in order to seriously apply the program which had been elaborated previously. The unification of the health system, the coordination of the education systems, and the organization of the State were the subjects of the first governmental decrees enacted.

We went through July, August, and September working without rest. There were no salaries and they paid each of us with a bag of food. The economic cell was set up, a replica of what had been a cell before the triumph. Some *compañeros* who had been in Costa Rica were there and we were joined by Emilio Baltodano[26] who had been in the internal front, William Hüpper[27] who had come in from Mexico, Alfredo Alaniz,[28] Félix Contreras,[29] Orlando Núñez,[30] and Alvaro Guzmán,[31] among others.

° *You were the director of INCEI. When did they name you Minister of Foreign Trade?*

On August 9, 1979 they named me the Minister of Foreign and Domestic Trade. At the beginning, I was in the INCEI because there was no ministry; it had to be organized. We worked with the idea of forming a ministry, and the recommendations we received from internationalist *compañeros* who had joined in the process had an influence on its organization. They recommended that there be a ministry in order to give more status to the country's trade policy, both foreign and domestic, and also in order to give importance to the role that planning should have in Nicaragua.

So I began work on forming the Ministry of Foreign and Domestic Trade with the criteria that trade should be conceived of in an integrated way. In that way, when we talked about basic grains, for example, we could market them domestically or abroad. That's how we built the Ministry of Foreign and Domestic Trade and we set up the companies which would specialize in executing both domestic and foreign trade policy.

° *When were the areas of foreign and domestic trade separated?*

At the end of 1979. We thought it prudent to separate the two areas. We considered it more important to dedicate more time to organizing the foreign trade apparatus. And so, in January 1980, the Ministry of Foreign Trade was formed.

° *Which countries did the new government first make contact with in order to receive financial support?*

The countries of Central America, Venezuela, and Mexico. The role of Mexico was extremely important throughout 1980, 1981, and 1982.

° *Were any conditions placed by these countries on the aid offered?*

None.

° *At the beginning, what were the financial and trade contacts with the government, banks, and companies of the United States like?*

The thing that stands out the most from 1979 was the dispute that arose with the Standard Fruit Company,[32] which led to a crisis that culminated with a decree in December 1979. This decree was interpreted by the transnational company as an action towards nationalization of its operation and blocking its functioning in Nicaragua. I would say that this was the most important confrontation in the first phase of the government.

The dispute with Standard Fruit showed some of the contradictions inside the Sandinista Front. Some saw confrontation as inevitable; others saw the possibility of restructuring the form of the relation that this transnational had with the banana sector. But it wasn't our intention to expel Standard Fruit. However, the reading they made of events, combined with the international situation of banana production, led them to pull out of Nicaragua.

° *What differences arose with the private sector when the Ministry of Foreign Trade as the regulatory body and the State-run trade concerns were formed?*

At that time, the private sector didn't express itself in a radical way against nationalization. I even named a businessperson by the name of José Antonio Baltodano[33] who had a great deal of experience in coffee as the first director of the ENCAFE company[34]—probably the most important company at that time. He had put forward arguments not to nationalize the international trading of Nicaraguan coffee, but over time, he was convinced of the need for nationalization to the point where he took charge of ENCAFE. At the beginning, a good part of the private sector understood the need for the transformations, but later, with the destabilizing offensive carried out by the U.S. government, the private sector began to come out against the revolution.

While the United States maintained its aid to Nicaragua—that lasted for almost a year and a half—the attitude of the Nicaraguan private sector was one of accepting the transformations that were being effected. Certainly, I don't mean to say that there weren't differences; there were.

I remember that at the beginning, all those officials who weren't guerrillas, who hadn't participated directly in military actions, were considered bourgeois. Because of that many contradictions arose, some of them fictitious. Resentment grew and lines of communication were broken. Nonetheless, Robelo, Violeta Chamorro, and Ramírez were always looking for a way to communicate with the different sectors in order to concretize the mixed economy that had been spoken of in the government plan.

When the United States adopted an aggressive attitude towards Nicaragua and opened centers for armed training in Florida, the situation in Nicaragua began to become polarized and the private sector protested that there was uncertainty, that we wouldn't let them work, that the productivity of labor had declined because the workers were always in meetings, that the State wanted to take over everything.

It's curious to note that the real representatives of capital, such as Pereira,[35] the Maríns,[36] Fernández Holmann,[37] and the Pellas group[38] which had been part of COSEP, left the country by 1981. Others, such as Hannon,[39] Mancel,[40] and Dreyfuss,[41] kept their distance from the positions of the new COSEP leadership although they didn't leave the country. Those who remained as the leaders were mid-level people with very little economic weight. Some weren't even businesspeople; maybe they were accountants in some company and their boss was with COSEP.

These people began to act against the revolution, driven by the enthusiasm that the U.S. government instilled in them. The COSEP members who went against the revolution are those that political analyst André Gunder Frank once called the "lumpen-bourgeoisie." They were the caboose of U.S. policy, people without capital and therefore those with the least amount of autonomy with which to stand up to the United States. They didn't have an entrepreneurial attitude nor did they have their own strategy of developing themselves as businesspeople in new circumstances. They became viscerally polarized.

° *What concrete effect did the the U.S. government have on these differences inside the Government of National Reconstruction? For example, how did it affect Robelo?*

Robelo began to lose enthusiasm from the moment the FSLN strengthened its organization. I remember well that when I was directly responsible to him in the Government Junta, he made critical comments about the Sandinista cells that were forming inside the ministries. According to Robelo, this was a kind of parallel government. I explained that such organizing was legitimate and explained the meaning of the cells to him, but he insisted that it was a way to obstruct the functioning of the Government of National Reconstruction.

Of course *Sandinismo* had a right to organize itself, to close ranks, especially considering that confrontation with the United States was getting closer. Robelo and Arturo Cruz[42] were isolating themselves. Both were people who were very vulnerable to pressures from the United States, and that in turn created distrust of them within the FSLN.

The cases of Robelo and Cruz have that specificity, but on the other hand, a criticism must be made of the sectors inside the FSLN who took the "class" point of view to the extreme, adopting an attitude that those who had been educated abroad or who weren't from the popular classes "would not go all the way."[43] These positions also caused economic and political damage.

° *Which professionals did you begin work with in the Ministry of Foreign Trade? What was your attitude towards the professionals who were working in the INCEI when the revolutionary government took power?*

I had an open attitude of making them feel welcome. I think that this attitude helped in the formation of a highly qualified work team in the Ministry.

If you look at the list of people who were on the payroll, you will find *compañeros* with a much higher academic level and with much more technical knowledge than those who were in the other State institutions in Nicaragua. That was part of the success of the foreign trade project; we were able to bring together capable and practical people.

III

Foreign Policy and the
U.S. Blockade

The importance of foreign policy

° *The social base which was developed to guarantee the
defense of the revolution was complemented by a very
efficient foreign policy that became a virtual wall of con-
tainment against U.S. aggression. Do you think that
Nicaragua's foreign policy was successful during the ten
years of the Sandinista goverment?*

Without a doubt. It was important in making clear the illegal-
ity, illegitimacy, and injustice of U.S. aggression against Nicaragua.
The participation in the Non-Aligned Nations, the use of the United
Nations as a forum to constantly denounce the attacks being made
against Nicaragua, the use of the International Court of Justice, and
the active role of the bilateral communication we developed with
the countries of Latin America, Europe, Africa, and Asia were
decisive in defending the country.

The fact that Nicaragua was elected to the U.N. Security
Council in the midst of the most open gestures of war by the United
States demonstrated our ability to build an international support
base. This was key to discouraging the United States from embarking on an adventure of direct intervention.

The contribution Nicaragua made to the formation of the Contadora Group[1]—a result of a meeting of Latin American foreign ministers in Nicaragua to try to find a Latin Americanist response to the conflict in the region—is more evidence of the active role our foreign policy played in the regional search for peace.

In addition, Nicaragua's contribution to Esquipulas[2]—even assuming commitments unilaterally—and the major role it played in the Non-Aligned movement were far-reaching diplomatic actions which helped contain the interventionist avalanche coming at us from the government and the political right-wing groups of the United States.

° *Within this foreign policy, what efforts were made to improve relations with the United States?*

After the 1990 elections, we had time to make an evaluation, not just of the election results, but also of the achievements we made and the errors we committed. The willingness of Nicaragua's government to normalize relations with the United States was indefatigable, and we made multiple efforts towards that goal. Nonetheless, we underestimated the magnitude of U.S. power.

In effect, we defeated the U.S. military strategy but we forgot that the policy of the United States was more than just one of purely military invasion. It had other powerful ways to apply pressure which were just as effective. I think our public discourse showed that we didn't understand this reality. That discourse was charged with an excessive amount of anti-U.S. rhetoric which contradicted the efforts at negotiation we were making. There wasn't a clear understanding that our enemy was much more powerful with its diplomatic and economic actions than in its military maneuvers.

° *Many of us from the Southern Cone of Latin America have been surprised at how, while surrounded by rightist regimes, it was possible for Nicaragua to maintain such close relations on the political and even business level with the rest of the countries of Central America. What efforts were made by the Ministry of Foreign Trade under your leadership to maintain relations with the business and governmental sectors of the rest of the countries of the region?*

In spite of the dramatic tensions that came up between us and our neighbors in Costa Rica, Honduras, and El Salvador, the ministers responsible for economic integration met at least twice a year, and we not only discussed economic themes but political ones as well. In 1987, before Esquipulas, we insisted on the need for the

Central American foreign ministries to reduce the tensions among themselves so that they could communicate.

My colleagues in the ministries of our neighboring countries didn't display the degree of communication that there was among the ministries responsible for economic integration. We even had a meeting in June 1987 in Pochomil[3] at which the five ministers responsible for economic integration were discussing a customs duties package and we ended up spending more than 24 hours on political themes.

The then-minister for El Salvador was arguing that Nicaragua should stop helping revolutionary movements, the FMLN[4] in particular. Guatemala and Costa Rica were stressing the need for the foreign ministers to communicate because there had been problems, in particular with the Nicaraguan Foreign Ministry. After the experience at Pochomil, they became convinced that there was a basis for asking that the presidents reopen the presidential dialogue.

The perseverance over the years of the ministers responsible for economic integration—Orlando Solórzano[5] played an important role—was the basis for opening up the road that later led to the signing of the Esquipulas I Accords in 1987. It showed that economic discussion could be a bridge to peace and could be a way to tackle political positions. I think the letter signed at Pochomil and sent to the presidents of Central American countries played an important role in encouraging the holding of the presidential meetings, which culminated with the Esquipulas accords.

The view we had in foreign trade left us somewhat isolated in the government. When I spoke with my cabinet colleagues about Central America, many thought it was incompatible to link Nicaragua, a revolutionary country, to the rest of the countries of the region, which had anachronistic structures. My position was that trade has no ideology. A good test of this idea was that countries like China and the Soviet Union were fervently looking to expand trade with the West.

Apart from that, my role as Minister of Foreign Trade was to maintain the flow of commerce with Central America. And, even if we had wanted to be against it, the degree of economic integration that the Central American countries already had made it virtually impossible to ignore the existence of these economic ties.

I'm convinced that the challenge of developing a small country like Nicaragua forces us to look at the neighboring countries. I defend Central American economic integration even though I have been critical of the very fragile basis on which it has been sustained. It's necessary to change and restructure that basis.

In short, my position with respect to the relations with Central America was very much in the minority, but over time, my position showed itself to be correct because trade, although reduced in volume, always continued to be significant, even at the most critical times that we had in getting supplies in Nicaragua. The *buhoneros*[6] who bought products in Central America and sold Nicaraguan products were the ones who could take the pineapple of La Concha,[7] papayas, and mangos to sell in the neighboring countries and at the same time supply the Nicaraguan market with products which otherwise wouldn't have entered the country because of a shortage of foreign exchange.

Furthermore, the flow of transport drivers up and down Central America kept the Nicaraguan border open and that allowed for Nicaragua to continue to be seen as part of the Central American isthmus even though it had a different ideology from the rest of the countries of the region. The lesson to be learned is that economic integration is not impossible even when there are political and ideological differences.

° *So economic policy has been decisive in the efforts for peace in spite of the ideological and political differences.*

That's it exactly. A political strategy must be accompanied by an economic strategy. If the economic groups—which in Central America are very disparate—had been given the chance to participate in the benefits and costs that the Contadora process implied, it would have been to the advantage of that Latin Americanist effort. Not only political wills would have been put into play, but also economic interests, which in many cases would have played a supporting role so that political projects could be completed.

If the Central American business sector had had an influence over the U.S. business sector, maybe the United States would have thought twice about the adventure it got itself involved in in Central America during the 1980's.

Nonetheless, no one in Nicaragua wanted to see the economic instrument as a real element of pressure for attaining political agreements. I think that this bridge was not used with all the required vigor. However, the United States did use it as part of its policy of showing strength in order to have important Central American business sectors join its side, giving them the business opportunities to provision the counterrevolutionary forces. Meanwhile, because we didn't give sufficient importance to the economic aspects of our relations with business groups in the area by developing traditional business arrangements, our chances to influence these sectors were reduced.

° *In what way were you affected by the U.S. pressure on Central American governments and businesspeople to isolate Nicaragua?*

The businesspeople were fearful of coming to Nicaragua. An image had been sold of a red Nicaragua where atrocities were committed and where there was no free enterprise. I vividly recall the first time that Honduran Minister of the Economy Reginaldo Panting[8] came to Nicaragua. I went to receive him at the border. His first words were, "My wife says I'm crazy to come to Nicaragua." I took Panting to different places in Nicaragua, among them the Sébaco Valley[9] where an agro-industrial complex was being built. He spoke with campesinos who were part of that project and he left pleased. We went all over the country, and at the end of his visit he told me that, in reality, what he'd seen was a lot different from what he'd read in the Honduran press.

It should be pointed out that when we were speaking with the ministers about economic integration, no one hid the fact that there were U.S. pressures, but they were worried about what would be said when they returned to their country. The propaganda of terror promoted by the United States through its information service was a very important aspect of its "low-intensity" war strategy against our country.

The U.S. blockade

° *As you have noted, the trade and financial aspects of U.S. policy had a very important influence on Nicaraguan life. This activity, above and beyond the exclusively military activity, is what has been called "low-intensity warfare," which for many analysts had a very decisive role in the electoral defeat of the Sandinista Front.*

What measures were taken by the revolutionary government to confront this policy? Did the Sandinista government expect this reaction from the United States? Was it prepared to act in an agile way when faced with the U.S. government's economic measures to place obstacles in the way?

I think in this respect that the Cuban experience was very useful for us since they always stressed the need for us to be prepared so that what had happened to them wouldn't happen to us, and so that we wouldn't be taken by surprise. We prepared legal, financial, and trade actions for the eventuality of an outbreak of this so-called "low-intensity" warfare.

In the Ministry of Foreign Trade, we took measures beginning in 1981 as part of the trade policy to defend the revolution. We diversified markets and formed companies abroad which—it should be pointed out—always belonged to the government of Nicaragua.

Although we put down our own names as front men[10] in order to charter them abroad, immediately after they were set up, the corresponding shares were handed over to the office of the Attorney General[11] of the Republic so that there wouldn't be the slightest doubt that these companies responded to the defense of the nation's interests and were not for making individual business deals.

We began by opening a trade office and, later, a trade company in Spain. Then we set up another in Panama and another in the United States. In that way, we were developing instruments which would work to be able to channel trade in a diversified manner and to create alternative conditions in case of any eventuality. In this way, if the trade embargo was to materialize—as it did in May 1985—the companies abroad would be the instrument with which to confront it.

In the financial system, measures were also taken so that the accounts which Nicaragua had abroad wouldn't be discovered. In this way, there was preparation, but I think that the process of confrontation begun by the United States was rapid and didn't leave much time to make things better.

But yes, in effect, we made prior preparations and that mitigated the effects of the embargo. I want to talk here about the experience, for example, that we had with the withdrawal of the Standard Fruit operation from Nicaragua.

°   *Yes, tell us about the "banana operative." I remember we were together at Harvard University in April 1985 and you took part in a discussion about the "case" of the banana. The banana marketing operative that the Nicaraguan government set up was recognized as successful in academic circles. Why was that so?*

First, because bananas have been one of the myths imposed on Latin America throughout the years. The myth says that to market them, a transnational corporation is needed. The fact that a small country set up a structure to be able to market its own bananas was seen as unprecedented. This attracted the attention of the international academic community because the experience of that marketing, with our own resources, not only gave Nicaragua the freedom to supply the product and negotiate better prices, but also gave it the freedom to establish a structure which other countries normally don't want to set up for fear of countermeasures from the transnationals. The fact of having broken through this fear, even before the trade embargo was declared, was one of the things noted by the academic world.

I think that the experience of our entry into the U.S. market after the withdrawal of Standard Fruit was extremely positive and gave a lesson to the rest of the countries of Latin America. I also believe that once the economic embargo was imposed and it was impossible to take the product to the United States, the rapid and agile fashion in which we acted to send the product to Europe—a market totally unfamiliar to us—was also a show of audacity and organizational ability that was worthy of international recognition.

° *Prior to the generalized embargo of May 1985, in 1983 the U.S. Department of Trade substantially reduced the sugar quota, which gave preferential prices in the U.S. market. Obviously, this was an important loss because Nicaragua no longer received that additional benefit. How was this problem dealt with? Did the new buyer countries pay a price similar to what the United States had been paying?*

At first, the buyers of Nicaraguan sugar were Arab countries: Algeria, Libya, and Iran. Those countries paid us preferential prices, not to the same extent that the U.S. market had been paying, but at least it cushioned the effects imposed by restricting the sugar quota to the U.S. market a little.

These agreements to supply sugar to some Arab countries allowed us to have a source of petroleum resources which Nicaragua could sell on the international market, a task which I ended up coordinating. In this way, we were trying to assure more liquidity for the economy in order to confront the blockade and the limitation on credit from the international banks.

° *Aside from sugar and bananas, both important products in the U.S. market, the May 1985 blockade affected other products, principally meat, seafoods, and tobacco. Is there something worth noting with respect to the sales strategy and marketing alternatives for these products?*

We wanted to assure that there would be markets for those products and, to that end, the companies which had been set up abroad allowed us to penetrate new markets in Western Europe and Canada. Back when we could still export to the U.S. market, marketing structures were being developed in the United States that allowed us to make contacts with other suppliers of meat and seafoods operating from the United States. When the embargo was imposed, what we did was transfer our marketing operation from the United States to Canada. And later, we penetrated the European market by way of another company that we had set up previously. In that way, new sources of financing opened up which were very important from 1985 on.

The pre-exportation credits allowed us to finance economic activities that the international banks didn't give us funding for. Through this route, resources materialized from being granted credits for a year on account in exchange for our guarantee to deliver products such as coffee, cotton, sugar, meat, and seafoods. This form of trade turned out to be expensive, but since there was no alternative, we had to opt for it.

°   *In part, you have responded to my questions about the effects of the foreign trade blockade. At that time, there was a great deal of concern that the U.S. government would freeze Nicaraguan accounts in the branches of U.S. banks in other parts of the world. What alternatives were implemented by the Nicaraguan government to deal with the embargo on imports and the possible embargoing of bank accounts?*

Prior to the embargo, the accounts that Nicaragua had abroad were being handled in code and through different banks in different countries. Financial operations were triangulated so that the resources wouldn't be out in the open. This was done under the control of the Central Bank.

In the Ministry of Foreign Trade and the companies under my responsibility, we handled only those resources that originated from the Clearing House[12] operations. In the import operations, we made use of "triangular" arrangements which allowed the country to get supplies of some products which are only made in the U.S. market. As a norm, we avoided having any company belonging to the ministry get involved in triangulation operations, even though the blockade was absolutely illegal.

During my work in foreign trade, we extended Nicaraguan trade to Taiwan, China, Korea, Eastern countries, and Western Europe. There wasn't a country where we weren't making some kind of effort, and a vast network of contacts was developed abroad during the ten years of our government.

° *What was the reaction of Nicaraguan businesspeople to the U.S. blockade? Did they reject it because of its economic effects, or was it more fashionable to believe that the blockade would destabilize the Sandinista government?*

The real capitalists—those who actually owned productive assets— expressed rejection, but the politicized sector of the business groups which had used the cover of the business organization for political ends applauded this measure taken by the U.S. government, showing their anti-national spirit.

° *What was the reaction of U.S. businesspeople who up to that date had had business dealings with the Nicaraguan government? I remember that in April 1985, days before the embargo, I went with you to the United States and you lobbied in the universities and among business and political groups.*

The maintenance of a link, of fluid communication with business sectors in the United States, and also with Central American businesspeople, is something I consider to be very important. On a number of occasions, meetings were held with high-level representatives of U.S. private enterprise as well as with businesspeople from the most diverse countries.

However, despite our efforts, the U.S. business groups that had had dealings with us until 1985 saw themselves forced to change their strategy as a result of the embargo. Some stopped doing business, but others continued to trade with Nicaragua through third parties, by third routes. I think that little by little these people, now that the embargo has been lifted, will renew business dealings with Nicaragua.

° *What was the reaction in international agencies to the embargo imposed on Nicaragua?*

I think it was one of impotence in the face of the empire. They considered that the government of the United States was violating agreements it had signed, including the GATT[13] or of the International Court of Justice, and others noted that those confrontations with Nicaragua had become of such a magnitude that there was little room left for international agencies.

I think that the international agencies showed they don't have the appropriate instruments to protect the interests of small countries. This gives rise to the urgent demand for a new international legal and economic order in which the rules of the game are respected independent of the size and political ideology of any country.

° *The U.S. blockade was a breaking point in which the acute shortage of liquid hard currency that had been affecting the country was made more severe. This led Nicaragua to intensify trade relations with the countries of Eastern Europe, in particular the Soviet Union.*

To what degree did the commitment with the Soviet Union in political and economic terms become more evident after the U.S. trade blockade? What did this extension of trade mean, and what were the limitations faced by Nicaragua because of its greater dependence on new credit lines and technologies different from those of the United States?

The U.S. embargo effectively forced a more acute dependence on the countries of the East, more than was originally intended. For my part, I always thought that our way around the blockade should be found in Latin America, but unfortunately, the crisis of the 1980's made it impossible for even the richest countries of Latin America to be able to commit resources to Nicaragua in the amounts and at the times they were required. Therefore, we had to increase our economic dependence on the Soviet Union especially, and on the countries of Eastern Europe, such as the German Democratic Republic and Bulgaria, and also on Cuba.

Great inconveniences were created with the extension of trade towards the East, but without a doubt, it was better than remaining completely isolated. Changing technologies were a big challenge for the national economy and meant we were frequently running short of spare parts. Nevertheless, the substantial contribution that those countries made in providing petroleum, as well as the contribution of hard currency that the U.S.S.R., the German Democratic Republic, and Cuba gave us, has to be acknowledged.

° *Besides the countries of the East, would you single out any European or Latin American country that demonstrated a particular solidarity to Nicaragua in those difficult times?*

Without a doubt the Nordic countries, particularly Sweden, played an outstanding role of solidarity. In addition, Spain, Holland, and Italy merit special attention, especially in the last few years. Latin America expressed its solidarity with Nicaragua through Argentina, Peru, Venezuela, and Mexico. But it's necessary to point out that those countries faced serious limitations in resources, and some faced their own very deep crises that didn't allow them to aid Nicaragua to the extent that we required.

IV

Economic Decisionmaking
and Centralism

° *In almost all revolutions, serious economic errors have been committed in the first years of government. A lack of concern for fiscal and financial discipline and for exchange rate policies have led to problems in other areas. In Nicaragua's case, what lessons were learned from the economic decisions of the first years?*

The first years of government and the decisions adopted then were marked by a great deal of enthusiasm and a certain amount of paternalism toward the masses. The best lesson we can draw from this is that the economy and society aren't developed with paternalistic attitudes. Nonetheless, it must be recognized that this behavior by the government to a large extent reflected the great lack of experience we had in governing. It should be noted that none of the leaders of the revolution had academic training or experience as economists. Those who did have some theoretical training had it in other areas.

In reality, we had very little knowledge of economic management: Many measures implemented at the beginning later proved to be counterproductive in the long run. Some measures became a dead weight and resulted in an accumulation of enormous pressures which, together with the war, were responsible for the policies of stabilization and adjustment that we had to implement later. These included policies of very open credit and of overvaluing the *córdoba.* Some *compañeros* in the government didn't want to recognize the existence of the Central American Common Market,[1] something which even led them to the point of saying that as long as the Clearing House was open, we didn't have to worry about importing massively from Central America.

So, the first three years saw massive growth of imports, with a significant portion of the goods coming from Central America, and that resulted in a big debt to all the countries of this sub-region being accumulated from the beginning of the revolution.

In the area of credit, there wasn't a banking attitude, but rather one of wanting to make that monetary instrument reach all parts of the country. The government wanted to open bank branches all over the country, and financial resources were brought in by small plane to the farthest flung places.

Nobody at that time thought of directing those resources towards increasing production and making it more efficient. And who was ever concerned about bringing what was produced out from those far flung places? The watchword of democratizing credit predominated, and making credit effective for the whole of the country's economic activity went under separate cover.

The exchange rate was also overvalued, making the economic agents consider hard currency as something with no importance. This created the immense maladjustments in domestic prices which increased the demand for hard currency—a demand that couldn't be met—producing discrepancies between the official, parallel, and black money markets. This introduced a profound imbalance in favor of commercial activity, and productive activity declined. Therefore, in the midst of the crisis and shortages, small groups of businesspeople managed to make their capital grow, taking advantage of this anomalous situation.

I would add that there also was a fairly triumphalist attitude and an idea that resources would always be available to Nicaragua. The ability to procure resources from abroad in the first years of the revolutionary government infused us with false optimism. Substantial amounts of resources were obtained then which were quickly used up, rather than being assigned to sectors which could have made the economy recover rapidly.

Also at that time, a high degree of labor indiscipline prevailed and we didn't make the effort to contain it. This situation was maintained up until 1983-84 when we realized that labor discipline in the countryside had fallen to such an extent that the maximum workday was only three or four hours.

The fashionable ideology then among economic policy makers was that the revolution, in and of itself, was the source of benefits, so more effort to expand the country's productive capacity wasn't made. Some workers considered work to be a secondary thing. All this was part of the revolutionary enthusiasm and a partial view which led to an overly liberal conduct in the administration and use of resources, as well as in the willingness to work.

In those years, there also was an extremely distributionist thesis. According to that view, a skewed distribution of resources was the prime factor in the economy's failure to meet human needs. Therefore, the revolution was made by the poor in order to improve the living conditions of the poor, but the efforts to redistribute wealth were not complemented by the creation of a more disciplined workforce, an increase in the productivity of the worker, or an increase in overall production.

The fundamental problems at the beginning of the revolution were false optimism, a great deal of inexperience, and very little appreciation of the limits imposed by an economic process which, when faced with international reality, was going to have to demand efficiency and productivity. I think that the production level in 1980-81 happened by a miracle, not because great efforts had been consciously made to keep the economic pie from shrinking. In fact because we failed to make those efforts, year by year, that pie was getting smaller.

But besides all that, I sincerely believe that throughout the period 1980-87, policy makers maintained an erroneous position of separating the political front from the economic front. The economy was seen as technical; political issues were seen as distinct. It took a lot of time for the National Directorate to challenge this view.

° *And with respect to economic decisionmaking and planning?*

There were opposing theories about how to stimulate development. Some people emphasized Eastern European-style centralized planning. The participation of outside consultants from Cuba and the countries of Western and Eastern Europe had a lot of influence in this. I think that in the economic field, at the beginning of the government, we lost a bit of that characteristic which had led us to victory: the ability to devise things ourselves and not copy other people.

We made many mistakes as a result of copying from some frameworks which in practice turned out to be unsustainable for us. In addition, the insistence on State regulation in Nicaragua ran up against a shortage of human resources which totally prevented our being able to go ahead with centralized planning.

The State centralism that prevailed in the first years served to increase tensions with producers, and some of them became less interested in producing. This was so not just with big producers, but with medium and small producers too, some of whom later took up arms and joined the counterrevolution.

The paradox existed that while these centralist conceptions about the economy prevailed, there were important people at the decisionmaking level of economic policy who weren't Sandinistas and that complicated things even further. It was obvious then that the presence of Alfonso Robelo and Arturo Cruz would increase differences *vis-à-vis* the positions being put forward by the central planners.

The truth is that in those times of revolutionary euphoria, some people, looking through a skewed prism, had a high opinion of themselves as being the guarantors of the purity of revolutionary theory while they viewed those with more orthodox views through an extremely critical prism. It was part of the environment of the time in which some thought themselves to be revolutionaries because they argued for the short-term establishment of socialism and central planning. Meanwhile, others who were pragmatic and who didn't believe in Cuban-style socialism either worked on a subordinate level or simply didn't dare to enter fully into discussion about the economy for fear of opening fissures in the political unity of the FSLN.

In fact, in the first stage of the revolutionary government, economic themes were generally avoided because party leaders wanted to focus on reorganizing the social base by promoting programs with a social character. The economic front was considered secondary.

° *You speak of the influence of Cuban specialists. That surprises me because when I was working in foreign trade and later in planning, the truth is I never saw any Cuban economists near those ministries.*

The case of foreign trade was an exception. I remember the first meeting I had with the Cuban delegation in 1979 when we contacted them. My goal wasn't to have them send me advisors for the ministry, but rather to develop a program of visits to Cuba that would allow us to know about the experience of that country, an experience which I considered very important in the area of foreign trade.

I saw the Cuban experience as important but not determinant. In the first four or five years of the revolution this view made some FSLN leaders distrust me and the projects we were developing in the Ministry of Foreign Trade. Some thought my insistence on independence, on maintaining distance from the influences of the countries with central planning, showed a lack of conviction about building socialism.

In the Ministry of Foreign Trade we encouraged trade relations with Cuba, the U.S.S.R., East Germany, Bulgaria, and the rest of the socialist countries. But there were problems with how we implemented policies on trade relations, assigning responsibility for them among members of the FSLN National Directorate. I think the argument that they should be handled politically was correct at that time, although it caused tensions in the technical apparatus of the State. This situation was cleared up in 1985 when the Ministry of Foreign Cooperation[2] was formed, with Comandante Henry Ruiz as its minister.

° *Regarding the appraisal you just made and the suspicions that some leaders had about the Ministry of Foreign Trade, I have a question about a proposal which came up in the middle of 1981. I had recently arrived at the ministry when, at the top level of the government, integration of the Ministries of Foreign Trade and Domestic Commerce was proposed, but the proposal was never enacted. I wonder why, however, the suggestion was made that the two areas be re-integrated?*

I don't think it was for technical reasons. There was political distrust. It should be added that such distrust was also directed towards many professionals. There was a big problem of communication with some members of the FSLN.

Personally, I went through a very difficult time. The differences that existed between Ruiz and I were talked about a lot in public. But I don't believe it was a personal problem: The proof is that after 11 years of working closely together, I have the highest regard for Ruiz.

The reality is that there were different views. One view held that centralized socialism was possible, and in the economic field, State control was extolled. On the other side was the view of a renewed socialism which would have as its central axis the interests of the great majorities, but which would be decentralized and which would give a realistic recognition to the role of the market. This renewed socialism also attributed importance to the State as director of economic policy and as an instrument to compensate for the injustices of the market, and which adapted itself to our cultural idiosyncrasies, too.

One of the most surprising things was the transformation in the centralist thought of Ruiz when he resolutely supported the turn in economic policy that had to be promoted beginning in 1988.

I was convinced that socialism could not be imposed mechanically, by decree. My point of view, I think, led to distrust and confrontation, but that never hurt me enough to make me give up.

° *Besides these different conceptions, wasn't there a certain rejection of those who had had professional training?*

There was a lack of confidence in technicians, in those of us who had professional training and had studied abroad. This lack of confidence resulted in more conflict after some people in whom the members of the National Directorate had a lot of confidence, like Alfredo César, resigned. César's professional training and class background accelerated the generation of contradictions and made it so that in 1983 and 1984, the lack of confidence in professional personnel that some members of the National Directorate had grew on the basis of the bad experience that they had had with people like Alfredo César.

César's resignation did a lot of damage to Nicaragua. He had been a *compañero* along the way, a *compañero* of revolution, but his personality and political aspirations led him into confrontation. His resignation not only delivered tools to the enemies of the revolution with which to attack it, but also created an atmosphere of differences inside the government. The gap grew between those who had a realistic line of Nicaraguan-style socialism, socialism *a la nica,* and those who wanted to implement centralized socialism in the short term.

The tag of social democrat with which my position was labeled was never removed because I never stopped saying what I was thinking. I think this is one reason why they listened to me at the level of the National Directorate; the passage of time and the experience of going through such difficult times together allowed these discrepancies and mutual concerns about distrust to be eliminated.

Nonetheless, damage was done by these "radical" stances, by this closed view that socialism could only be built with those who came from a popular class background and by following the historical experience of actually existing socialism. There was, for some, the idea that the petty bourgeoisie, sooner or later, would pull away from the revolution. History proved the opposite. Probably more *compañeros* with popular class backgrounds left the revolution than those who came from the petty bourgeoisie.

°   *Alfonso Robelo, Violeta Chamorro, and Arturo Cruz broke with the government in the first years. Later, Alfredo César, and Haroldo Montealegre,[3] among others, left. After César left, it was rumored that you would leave too because you also differed with the centralist conception in the economic area. Why did you stay and continue with your commitment to the FSLN rather than joining the opposition?*

I think the reason I persisted, have persisted, and will continue to persist inside *Sandinismo* is because I see it as the only real option for replacing the Liberal-Conservative parallel which has done so much damage to the country. The revolution and *Sandinismo* came from inside the people, from a profound sense of national independence and social justice. My Christian conviction and my political responsibility committed me deeply to this project.

For that reason I remain and for that reason I persist in the struggle. I will debate the differences inside the revolution and not outside of it. Although the very concept of social justice was perceived by some Marxist-Leninist Sandinistas as a social democratic term, I insist on using it, just as I fought for the construction of democracy and believed firmly in political pluralism.

I believe that *Sandinismo* is the only guarantee that the type of project that I want for my country will be constructed. While I didn't think that bureaucratic socialism was going to crumble in the countries of the East, I was convinced that that model did not fit our history or our reality.

I wasn't able to think that social justice, non-alignment, and a mixed economy were going to be encouraged by way of the State controlling all the shares. I disagreed and would continue to disagree with a conception of total State control of private property. I don't believe that is the way to social well-being, above all in countries which haven't passed through significant stages of accumulation and growth.

In reality, my disagreements never made me think of abandoning the discussion inside the Sandinista Front since I understood all this as a mutual process of apprenticeship. Nevertheless, I was subject to strong criticisms and they even set traps for me.

° *What traps are you referring to?*

Here is a story that is carved in my memory. After barely 12 months of being the Minister of Foreign Trade, a false accusation was made that I had acted in a liberal and incorrect manner when I authorized a member of the cabinet, who was also a coffee producer, to set the price for coffee. It was alleged that in this way, he and I had made lucrative personal profits; that was false and unacceptable. A top Sandinista leader even brought this out publicly on television and radio.

That leader, who didn't even know me at that time, appeared on television to say that they were going to investigate us thoroughly. The investigations were carried out and they had me under constant scrutiny for a long and arduous time. When my innocence and my correct behavior in the Sandinista Front were established, nobody referred publicly to my innocence, even though the ruling of the Comptroller General of the Republic[4] had demonstrated it. I interpreted this as an expression of a lack of trust, and later, on countless occasions, even ten years later, I remember that story.

During the last election campaign, the UNO opposition made the false accusation that I was one of the people who was administering the resources that the National Directorate members had supposedly taken from the coffers of the State. I demanded inside the National Directorate that we file a suit so that our names would be cleared as a legacy to our people and our children, and I reminded them that this defamation campaign of the opposition was reaped from not having adopted a clear and decided attitude about me ten years earlier.

This mutual ignorance from the early days of the work in the government has been overcome, and relations of friendship have left the mistrust behind.

° *Let's return to the question of outside influences, to the consultants in the economic field. Besides the Cuban influence in economic affairs, what kind of people had an influence on central planning which prevailed in the early years of the revolution?*

Some people coming from Latin America had very centralist conceptions. Others from Western Europe did, too. Coming from England, the Cambridge scholar Valpy Fitzgerald[5] stands out. He had the full confidence of some members of the National Directorate and he consistently influenced them and other *compañeros* high up in the State apparatus.

It seems to me that Fitzgerald saw the revolution as a bit like an experiment and he had a clear influence in that "State-izing" view. In particular, his influence was seen in the Ministry of Domestic Commerce. When the acute problems of shortages arose in the country, He had an influence in the introduction of the ration card. I think this was a result of practical inexperience and also of the incorrect advice of those who believed themselves to be the bearers of Marxism and "true socialism."

° *Let's go back to another aspect of economic decisionmaking. From a period of the extreme centralization of economic policy in the Central Bank during the Somocista period, we entered into a revolutionary stage in which a number of ministries had shared and not very well-defined responsibilities over economic policy and there was little or no coordination.*

Under such structural conditions, and with the abovementioned difference in views about what to do with the economy, the success of a ministry seemed very much linked to the ability of the minister to apply pressure on the president. Do you think it was an error to have modified the original role of the Central Bank and to create so many normative ministries to implement economic actions?

The following would have to be noted about this complex new economic structure which lacked coordination. In the first place, Ruiz was entrusted with encouraging the implementation of the idea that the country should go into a system of centralized planning. In the second place, the personality of some people who were responsible for suggesting the first restructuring of the State is important. Among these, it is necessary to single out Alfredo César.

Let's begin with the second point. When César arrived in Nicaragua on July 19, 1979, he assumed the post of Secretary to the Government Junta of National Reconstruction. An immense amount of authority and responsibility was given to him. He and a few of us thought that a Central Bank with total power over economic policy was not the most appropriate strategy. My reading of César is that he feared his power as Secretary of the Government Junta would be reduced if he had to deal with a Central Bank president as powerful and as respected as Arturo Cruz. This factor influenced his decision to transfer the original functions of the Central Bank to other ministries.

But there was also the ideological factor. I recall vividly when we were talking about this theme and we all argued that the Central

Bank could not have the power that this institution had had during the time of "Che" Lainez[6] or Roberto Incer.[7] Apart from that, because there was a collective leadership body like the National Directorate, economic policy had to be looked at as a sum of the actors and not just as the result of one person's ideas. In looking at things this way, there was also the fact that with members of the National Directorate in the government, it was easier to give each one a quota of power.

Another important element which helped this position was that the Ministry of Planning[8] was conceived of as having a lot of power to act. In fact, many of the activities carried out by the Central Bank were passed to the Ministry of Planning.

Today, 11 years later, I think this wasn't the best measure. Although it was reasonable to avoid an extreme concentration of power in the Central Bank, it should have continued to carry out some functions which were natural to it.

The reorganization we carried out meant losing a lot of technical personnel who transferred to other areas or left the country. Perhaps the weakening of the Central Bank also affected the efficiency of the financial system, something which is of primary importance when it comes to assigning resources.

° *In this complex framework, there must have been some coordinating body for the economic area in the first years of the revolution. Was some body of discussion institutionalized in order to make decisions? Who was in it and what methods were used for making decisions about economic policy and the structural reforms of the economy?*

The first coordinating body in the economic area was called the Economic Council. Participating in it were representatives of the financial sector, the workers, and the UNAG (National Union of Farmers and Ranchers), among others, and it was basically presided over by Dr. Ramírez. Afterwards, this body was transformed into what was called the National Planning Council (CNP).[9]

The National Planning Council was the body for reconciling different ministerial points of view, and had a much more dynamic role when President Ortega took over the leadership of it after the 1984 elections. From that time on, but above all during the 1988 economic adjustment, Ortega not only moderated and synthesized the different positions within the government, he also showed he was willing to fight to promote a given line of action about economic policy.

° *What role did popular organizations play in the formation of Sandinista economic policy?*

Popular organizations were definitely a determinant factor all throughout the period 1979-1990. I would even say that in the new Chamorro government, their role coninues to be extremely important, though they may adopt different tactics than before.

The contribution of the last ten years is starting to show results, and these results demonstrate the profound transformation of Nicaraguan society today. Popular organizations demand an active role in the decisionmaking process, reaffirming that the Sandinista Revolution introduced the mechanisms that advance democratic society in general.

Groups like the labor unions, UNAG, FedSalud, Anden, and UNADI continue to participate actively in *concertación,* and their presence continues to be influential. The present government may not like that the popular organizations have such an important role to play, but I think that it would be extremely difficult to irradicate their power. I value this achievement as one of tremendous importance for the future of a real democratic society.

° *You mentioned the disagreements you had in the strategic field with Comandante Ruiz who at that time was playing a major role in the economic area as the Minister of Planning.*

Nicaragua's economic structure, with a wide range of small and medium producers, made it difficult to implement centralized plans, and made clear the need to actively utilize the instruments of economic policy.

There was a belief that Somoza was the owner of the whole country when in truth, the expropriation of the properties of Somoza and his followers really only affected between 30 percent and 40 percent of production, and in the countryside, less than 20 percent of the property, something important but not extraordinary. Earlier diagnoses that had been made and the views that some had about the economic structure of the economy created the illusion that by expropriating Somoza's properties, the State would be all-powerful and could regulate the economy without any hindrances.

However, as was shown in practice, the nationalization of the dictatorship's properties represented only a part of the properties of the country. It also wasn't understood that economic agents, independently of their size, respond with more agility to market forces than to a plan which tells them to produce, what products to produce, and when to produce them. Although I wasn't in favor of total economic liberty, I did think that we stripped the economic agents of their initiative.

It would be unfair, however, to make an analysis looking at only one point in time and only presenting this perspective. The political leadership—and that was the way I read it—was more concerned with ensuring the survival of the revolution and guaranteeing its defense. The development of the social base was a central concern of the country's political leadership in order to safeguard the revolution and to defend against a foreseeable aggression.

It was considered that acting along strictly economic lines—focusing on productive efficiency, for example, with distribution as a secondary priority—also had its limits, since that focus would clash with the historic demands that the people were making for health, education, social security, housing, etc. Indeed, the attempt made in the first years of the revolution to satiate those demands with subsidies from the national budget helped develop the social base that ensured the defense of the country.

I don't want to defend that stand, but I do think it's fair to put the facts and the concerns about the forthcoming aggression in a balanced perspective. Perhaps it would not have been possible to defend the country if there hadn't been a grassroots conviction in the revolution and its government. In this way, many measures taken in the first years were somewhat populist and didn't respond to an economic logic but rather to a more political logic.

Placing a priority on politics and defense meant that the model of centralized planning run into serious problems in later years. For example, towards the end of 1984, in order to strengthen the grassroots base in the countryside, we decided to distribute lands to campesinos from the Area of People's Property (APP),[10] to liberalize the prices of basic grains, and to eliminate the roadblocks checking for the illegal transfer of produce from one region to another. All these were measures adopted to safeguard the social base of the revolution and the defense of the country. And all those measures, in practice, broke with the centralist conceptions and with State control of the economy.

   °   *Defense and foreign policy defined the concerns of the leaders for obvious reasons. But I have the impression that the FSLN National Directorate avoided economic themes because of the differences and eventual ruptures that it could cause. State and market notions of pricing, the road*

to socialism, the questions raised by technologies, big en-
terprises or small-scale production, the role of campesinos
and workers, etc. were all crucial topics which gave rise to
the division of the FSLN into its three factions. What is your
opinion?

Now that you have put forward the thesis, I must say that I agree in part with you. I think that the National Directorate has maintained an extraordinary unity, and that unity has been possible thanks to a balance in the discussions. In fact, no document critical of the economic situation had receptivity at that time.

Comandante Daniel Ortega, little by little and above all from 1984 on, took on a more active role as coordinator of the National Directorate Political Commission,[11] and that's when there was more leadership in the process of transformation. In effect, many things were not proposed or could not be implemented in time due to the need to maintain the Front's unity. Perhaps it would have been technically correct to open up discussion about the themes of economic policy and development strategy, but while we were confronting an enemy as powerful as the United States, flanks couldn't be opened in our own camp, and that in part explains Ortega's tendency to put off discussions in which big differences of opinion would be aired.

Discussions in the economic field were put off until we found ourselves in an unsustainable situation of runaway inflation in the second half of 1987 and it became clear that the economic theme had an influence even on national security. The president then decided to lead this type of discussion more energetically. So from that moment on, the differences which people were afraid to deal with before were being put forward with more clarity.

But even so, I would say that for some time Ortega played the role of the devil's advocate with respect to our proposals to fight inflation. We should recall that in 1988 when the adjustment program had been in effect for 11 months, and we put forward the need to radicalize the program, we had to take part in long discussions with the National Directorate. In these, Ortega, after much reflection, accepted the program and later convinced the members of the National Directorate that the economic program should be adopted fully as proposed.

This experience, in which President Ortega's great ability to harmonize differences was demonstrated, is still alive for me.

Agrarian policy

° *Some economic errors are more serious than others. In Nicaragua's case, according to national and international specialists, the agrarian policy had a very negative effect on the political plane. Some small producers have pointed out that the policy of the Ministry of Agriculture and Agrarian Reform was oriented in favor of those who have always been favored, the producers of the Pacific, and that there was a lack of concern for the producers in the interior of the country. What is your appraisal of this?*

I don't agree that the agrarian policy was deliberately oriented to favor the producers of the Pacific. But I do agree that the big projects were a mistake. I never believed in the big projects and I continue not to believe in them. I don't believe in the ability to bring together all the production that you want to bring together. Nor do I believe that with big investments we were going to solve the problems of Nicaragua.

I think that the structure of ministerial delegates of the president in the regions,[12] with their corresponding sectoral delegates, was a negative experience for the country. Barely justifiable land interventions were made based on recommendations from delegates who didn't know the territory. State production units were created that weren't brought about in the best way, and this had negative consequences on the population's perception of what the regional delegates were doing, although I think there were some exceptions.

We erred in not being sufficiently self-critical about what we were doing with agriculture. The agricultural policy was skewed in favor of a greater State role and was centered on the idea of carrying out big projects and centralizing resources which could have been better invested in activities more in line with the reality of the country's economic structure.

The consolidation of the revolution's campesino social base —which was being badly damaged by the war since 1982-83— would have been more likely with a different policy.

I wouldn't hesitate to acknowledge that I confronted these policies insistently and openly, even though I have a high personal regard for Comandante Jaime Wheelock as I do for the other members of the National Directorate.

° *What were the major acheivements of the Sandinistas with*
regard to the integration of the Atlantic Coast?

I had few responsibilities as Minister of Foreign Trade, or later
as Minister of Planning, with the situation in the Atlantic Coast.
During most of the Sandinista period, all policy decisions related
to fishing and wood production in the coastal area were decided
and implemented in Managua, and the people of the Atlantic Coast
had little autonomy. In the later years, autonomy status was given
to this area, along with the question of how they would be able to
exploit their own natural resources without having to consult
Managua. This subject is still under discussion, but I am not sure
that solutions are still being sought.

I believe that our actions in the Atlantic Coast were insufficient in helping the peoples of those regions dramatically improve
their social conditions. Granting autonomy status to the Atlantic
Region was a bit step forward, but only the beginning of a process
of addressing the complexities posed by different cultures and
values.

In the first years of the Revolution, due to our overenthusiasm
and lack of experience, a great number of mistakes were made in
dealing with the peoples of the Atlantic Coast. We did not want to
accept that the cultural values of the Miskitos, Sumos, or Ramas
were consistent with our own vision of building a revolutionary
nation. Cultural contradictions arose, and the space for confrontation with them was opened.

It took us a long time to understand that these people could
also be as revolutionary as we were, although not necessarily in the
ways we wanted them to be. We finally acknowledged that the
specific characteristics of Atlantic Coast cultures required different
tactics, but in the meantime many wounds were inflicted, wounds
that will need time to heal.

V

Economic Policy

Years of plenty and macroeconomic tensions

° *Up until 1983, one could say that the Nicaraguan economy*
was going along reasonably well. We experienced a good
rate of growth compared to the rest of Central America and
an expansion of social services, which brought Nicaragua
a great deal of international recognition. However, in 1984
and 1985, the severe strains caused by the expansion of
credit, the increase in investments, and government expen-
ditures for the development of social programs and, later,
for military defense, became obvious.

Taking these elements into consideration, could you
make an assessment of the positive and negative aspects of
the period prior to the first economic adjustment in 1985.

On the one hand, we had to build up a national army which
would guarantee the stability of the revolution. In that respect, this
was a very important achievement. Nonetheless, a large amount of
resources were required to build up the army and I think that those
financial demands should have been appraised more carefully.

Throughout those ten years, we never made this kind of
appraisal. We were afraid to do it because to raise that kind of
objection, in one way or another, would be interpreted as not
placing enough priority on defense.

A big lesson to draw from that period is that even when priority is placed on something, there has to be a limit. I think that we went too far in building up the armed forces, security apparatus, and police. We created institutions for another type of country.

We needed a force capable of dissuading an interventionist adventure, but for all the investments that we made, I never thought that we were going to be able to prevent an intervention on the basis of our military forces alone.

It was thanks to the mobilization of the people and thanks to the promotion of social programs that a solid social base was created to prevent a U.S. invasion. The spirit of struggle was to be found more in the people defending their own gains than in building up structures that restricted resources and the possibilities for developing this social base.

° *Was it ever proposed that the army produce and not just consume?*

Yes, it was proposed many times. But this proposal ran contrary to military doctrine that prioritized preparations for the situation of aggression.

° *In February 1985, there was a certain modification of the central aspects of economic policy. An attempt was made to make the market and other indirect mechanisms prevail in order to orient economic activity. But if the war, as you pointed out, was the most important factor in explaining the maladjustments in the economy, why wasn't a war economy put into effect then?*

There wasn't clarity about what a war economy would mean—whether a war economy was interpreted as abandoning the model of the mixed economy, or whether it meant turning inwards. In reality, there wasn't the will to push for a sharp turn away from the idea that there should be a mixed economy. So to go into a process of a war economy was visualized as too big a step away from the strategic conception of the revolution. The idea that the Sandinista Front saw the mixed economy as a strategic issue was reaffirmed, even though many members still thought that this was a strictly tactical issue.

Lean years and the 1985 adjustment

° *In 1984, the economic situation was very difficult. There was an enormous fiscal deficit that was more than 20 percent of the Gross Domestic Product, an absurdly overvalued exchange rate, a financial deficit which resulted from surprisingly negative interest rates, and a trade deficit which was growing every year. The large macroeconomic gaps encouraged an increase in inflation, bringing as a consequence a decline in real wages and the development of the black market.*

In fact, the 1985 economic plan was a self-criticism of the previous years. President Ortega himself justified this new economic policy by saying, "If we've made a mistake, it's to have wanted to do everything all at once without taking into account the extreme limitations on the resources of the country." What were the main differences inside the FSLN around the turn made in economic policy in 1985?

It took a lot of time to implement the 1985 adjustment because the idea prevailed that we were preparing ourselves to deal with an aggression and that it was fundamental to build a social base willing to defend the revolution. Therefore, to make noise about the economy was seen as contradictory to creating these better social and material conditions. Those political criteria prevailed, and besides, the election campaign was being prepared.

When the FSLN won the 1984 elections, very few months passed before the National Directorate became convinced that we were reaching the bottom of the barrel. Our isolation was increasing and international aid wasn't flowing in in the amounts that it had flowed in before. This reality forced the National Directorate to accept the need to act on the central aspects of the economy.

It was an error to postpone the measures until February 1985. Likewise, the shallowness of the measures was an error. The lesson must be drawn that putting off economic problems and returning to them later forces the need for such harsh measures, measures that will always be in contradiction with the goal of protecting the well-being of the majority social strata of the population.

Beginning in September 1983, the economic cell which had been working at the beginning of the triumph began to function again. In it were Dionisio Marenco, Emilio Baltodano, Orlando Núñez, William Hüpper, Roberto Gutiérrez,[1] Ramón Cabrales,[2]

Néstor Avedaño,[3] and I. Support was given from advisors like Valpy Fitzgerald, Xavier Gorostiaga,[4] and Alban Lataste,[5] among others. There were different positions about how to go ahead with an economic policy without abandoning the basic elements of centralism which had prevailed.

The differences between those who didn't believe in strict controls and those with the centralist conception were expressed more clearly there. However, while the need to reduce the fiscal deficit was being discussed, we decided to go ahead with the Patriotic Military Service (SMP). That brought on an increase in defense expenditures and made it difficult to reduce fiscal spending. So the discussions of this working group centered a lot on the informal sector and how to avoid placing even more obstacles in the way of formal economic activity.

°   *These new ideas were an attempt to have the instruments of economic policy and the role of the market prevail over material balances and State centralism. Why did this new policy fail?*

The war was the most decisive factor in preventing the 1985 adjustment from producing the expected results. At that time, the military activity of the counterrevolution increased. Moreover, the May 1985 embargo was being clearly felt. I think that I was somewhat triumphalist back in 1985 when I was saying that the embargo wouldn't have serious effects because we already had well-diversified markets.

The embargo, nonetheless, had a very great impact in 1985 and 1986, causing shortages of spare parts. We lacked resources for the rapid replacement of the existing technology of the country. The embargo seriously disrupted the effort to make an economic adjustment and imposed a logic of survival more than a logic of stability. The 1985-87 period was very limited in terms of getting supplies, even though we tried to free up the market.

The informal market expanded dramatically, and while the government was working on the formal sector, the informal economy set its own game rules.

°   *Why did the government persist in maintaining a policy of absurdly negative interest rates which didn't necessarily favor the social base of the revolution and instead favored the wealthiest sectors with credit? Why did the government insist on an exchange-rate policy which overvalued the córdoba enormously? Was the active non-utilization of these instruments due to a fear that inflation would be exacerbated, or was there another reason?*

It wasn't a lack of understanding of these phenomenona. Besides the difficulties caused by the war, ideological differences came into play. Both the agricultural and industrial sectors were influenced by institutional interests and a lot of political power. Interest rates were of concern to the ministries in those sectors. They used the respectable position of defending the small producer, but it wasn't said clearly that the big sector of the Area of People's Property (APP) was being defended, too.

Obviously, no one was thinking of giving benefits to the big capitalists, but there definitely were important authorities persistently defending their institutional powers and the APP companies which had been created. If a given product which was of interest to a sector had higher costs, these powerful producers fought for higher prices, which ended up favoring capitalist sectors.

To have maintained the practice for so long that—on top of having Comandantes of the Revolution in charge of them—ministries had companies under their administration made it impossible to see clearly where the overall interest began and where the particular interest of the sector ended.

I feel that given the close link between the government and the party, it wasn't the most prudent thing to have Comandantes of the Revolution in charge of State ministries. It was problematic to have government economic policies enacted by the powerful top leaders of the party. This made it more difficult to have a coherent management of economic policies. Unfortunately, this theme was always one which was taboo and nobody wanted to touch it.

° *So you don't agree with the systematic policy carried out by the revolution of forgiving the debts of the APP and other producers.*

It shouldn't have been a generalized policy: It should have been case by case and selective. You can not underestimate the importance that credit plays or the importance of efficiency—so that the producers work, work profitably, and can meet their financial commitments. The new concept of banking in which credit didn't just favor landowners was valuable. However, we should have designed some instruments that would work to reward efficiency and production, but not at the cost of taking land away from campesinos.

The credit policy ended up being a reward for not producing, and a cover-up for the inefficiency of the very structures which we had created.

° *Didn't the ministers discuss the inefficiencies of the APP? Weren't they concerned that the problem was getting worse over time?*

Yes, they were. But it always ended with the comment, "This is *political*."

The informal sector

° *The pricing policy applied until 1984 affected the campesinos and many times made it so they wouldn't sell their products to the State institutions and they would instead sell directly to the black market. Also, this time saw an intense development of the black market for the dollar. In this way, the informal sector of the economy was strengthened.*

At first, the policies of controlling commerce pushed some ministers to repress the informal sector, but later—in particular since 1985—there was an attitude of acceptance towards it. How can these contradictions be explained?

It was clear that the informal sector, in the midst of a situation of an extreme shortage of resources, was called on to play an important role. This consideration was in direct opposition to the desire to formalize the economy. That's how I explain the different opinions stated in public by some Sandinista leaders who saw the informal sector as a threat.

In reality, there were good reasons for this fear since the underground economy was a constant challenge to the economic policy and to the structures of the formal economy of the country. However, their mistake was to apply inadequate policies to this sector, as well as going to the absurd extreme of applying repressive measures.

Because of this, that sector lined itself up against the revolution. The *buhoneros* and the merchants involved in informal activity came out very negatively against the revolution.

The 1988-89 adjustment

° *Macroeconomic imbalances increased in 1986 and 1987. By the end of 1987, the cumulative annual inflation rate was more than 1,300 percent and the maladjustment of relative prices was worsening. The government then decided to implement the 1988 Stabilization and Adjustment Program and a demonetization—taking money out of the economy by creating a new currency to fight inflation. What discussions were held about the new adjustment program?*

In our conversation, I've placed emphasis on how the perspective which separated economic aspects from political ones was a mistaken one. This came to be widely accepted as time went on.

Prior to the new adjustment, political agreements had been signed at Esquipulas. This opened up a window to the possibility for peace and, with that, there were greater possibilities to manage the economic affairs of the country in a decisive way. With the Esquipulas Accords as a background, it was possible to have a more meaningful influence over the deteriorating economic situation, which, in my opinion, was as big a threat as the counterrevolution.

The armed counterrevolution was a threat, but so were the big economic tensions and limitations. Because of this, Esquipulas was an important step in Nicaragua's history, a step which changed people's awareness and appreciation of the seriousness of the economic risks. The people's goal of peace helped the leaders of the revolution become convinced that the economic crisis and inflation, in particular, were eroding the social base.

The plan for demonotization and economic restructuring began to be discussed seriously. In its first phase, a strictly monetary action was taken with the so-called Plan Bertha.[6] Ortega and Sergio Ramírez, the armed forces, the police, and a large number of government officials were involved in that plan.

It should be noted that despite having so many people participate, it was the biggest secret ever kept by so many people. More than 60,000 Nicaraguans were mobilized in the demonetization operation.

Involved in its execution were—besides the Ministry of Planning—Dionisio Marenco, Dr. Joaquín Cuadra Chamorro, William Hüpper, Roberto Gutiérrez, Emilio Baltodano, and I, together with hundreds of other *compañeros* who gave the demonetization program its final form. Of course, the new bills had to be printed a long time in advance. So while Ruiz was Minister of Planning he played a major role in this plan.

   ° *Prior to 1988, was the possibility of a demonetization ever proposed? I ask this because it seems to me that towards the end of 1984, we discussed this topic.*

Since 1984, the idea came up. However, the National Directorate put Ruiz in charge of beginning that program; it was to be handled with the utmost secrecy. But I reiterate, only when the new conditions of peace were being opened up by Esquipulas did the theme of the economy begin to acquire relevance and, thanks to the work of Ruiz, the government had the new currency prepared.

The operation was prepared in the period from November 1987 to January 1988 and, in effect, I believe it was one of the most audacious actions ever taken by the revolution. I have always thought of the monetary reform as a demonstration of the great logistical and military capacity that we had attained. In addition, it was a lesson that when the question of sectoral powers is set aside and everyone works towards the same central goal, it is possible to make huge gains.

A similarly successful action was the construction of the Olof Palme Convention Center,[7] a project that was completed in less than six months and that, in the eyes of the world, was impossible to do given the scarce resources that Nicaragua had. Similarly, the National Literacy Crusade[8] and the Popular Health Campaigns[9] were very important actions in which the whole nation was committed. These kinds of actions show the potential that a country has when sectoral fiefdoms are eliminated and all sectors act towards a common goal under national coordination.

   ° *Some saw the demonetization process, eliminating the old currency, as a way to take liquid funds away from the counterrevolution and those who supported its financing. Is that how it was?*

That wasn't the main goal, at least not to my understanding. It was a complementary result since it was obvious that the counterrevolution was taking advantage of the disparities in the exchange rate in the official and black market. Both the armed counterrevolution and the opposition institutions were very much favored by the distortions in the price of hard currency. Because of that, the U.S. government could carry out its destabilization policy while spending very little in the way of resources.

° *Let's look at the substantive aspects of the February 1988
Stabilization and Adjustment Program. What were the
goals and the main areas of tension?*

The document we wrote in June 1988 contains the most
precise description of what we were after. There was recognition
that the economy had been damaged because of the war and the
blockade and also because of some ill-advised policies which had
been implemented in earlier years and which had still to be
reversed.

The drop in foreign trade, for example, had to be reversed. The
macroeconomic conditions for stimulating the recovery of production as a whole, and in particular export production, had to be
modified. The alarming maladjustment of prices where a gallon of
gasoline was cheaper than a dozen mangos, for example, had to be
corrected. The black market was also having an absurd effect on the
incentives to production and it was favoring minority economic
groups.

First, we tried to readjust relative prices; this was intimately
linked to the exchange-rate policy. The exchange-rate policy had
to be made into something more dynamic and realistic. Starting in
May 1988, we carried out currency devaluations which sought to
recover the profitability of exports and give a dose of realism to the
prices charged for imported goods and to the relation of prices for
goods produced nationally.

Second, the level of government expenditures was way above
our possibilities and so the fiscal deficit had to be cut drastically.

Third, we sought to eliminate the excessive administrative
controls which we had put on the economy.

Fourth, we tried to be more flexible with wages, allowing free
negotiations between companies and employees and overcoming
the rigidity of the National System of Organization of Labor and
Salaries[10] which distorted prices and wages greatly.

With these considerations in mind, the demonetization was
carried out first and, afterwards, prices were made more flexible.
Later, we exercised finely tuned control over public expenditures.
The process of monthly follow-ups that we made to the adjustment
program was very important, allowing us to fulfill many of the goals
we had proposed. At the same time, it allowed us to have an
influence over governmental coherency, little by little having the
ministries give up somewhat their monopolies and adapt themselves to the policy that was being drawn up in the National
Planning Council.

Once we entered into the process of adjusting prices by means of devaluations, we saw that it was important to define a framework for wage adjustments in the central government. In the first stage, we based that on the changes in price of a given list of basic goods.

° *Why, after having made such a radical response to the economic maladjustments with the demonetization, why did the ministers wait until June 1988 to apply all the necessary complementary measures? It seems to me that we lost precious time. It was only since June, and then in 1989, that there was a clear continuation of the economic policy. From that moment on, we saw the ministers in charge of the economic area meeting weekly with a technical team to evaluate and make adjustments to the economic policy.*

It's valid to separate out some points in time. After having placed the discussion of economic matters on the agenda, a vacuum was produced from February 1988 until June, a period in which political issues predominated over economic ones in the National Directorate's discussions. We lost a great opportunity to apply measures that should have been adopted immediately after the demonetization.

Let's remember that the restructuring of the government happened at the end of April 1988 and the beginning of May. From that moment on, we had periodic meetings of the National Planning Council in order to follow up on the economic policy. That was what the president asked me to do when he transferred me to the Ministry of Planning.

It's true that beginning in June 1988, we introduced many new economic measures including the liberalization of the economy, but let's note that in October, this effort ran into a totally extra-economic obstacle: Hurricane Joan.[11] The increase in fiscal expenditures and the additional credits given to the victims of the hurricane injected a considerable amount of pressure into the inflationary process; we ended up with an accumulated inflation rate of 33,000 percent by the end of 1988.

The arrival of Hurricane Joan was a disruption and confirms for me the thesis that the inflation we were experiencing was not just a question of excess demand and low production, but also one of the unreasonable expectations of the population given the circumstances.

Hurricane Joan forced us to increase spending for supplies and reconstruction in the aftermath of the storm. But more important than these expenditures was the fueling of inflationary expectations, above all because of the weak and timid response that the international community made in the wake of the catastrophe of the hurricane.

The population perceived that in spite of the efforts being made by the government, the economic situation was not going to be resolved because international co-responsibility in the form of aid wasn't there. We had to apply even harsher measures in 1989.

I have been accused on countless occasions of having given the economic program a character centered on aggregate demand and not so much on productive recovery. I was told I was being too neo-liberal, or like the International Monetary Fund, even though, in reality, my perspective went beyond the strictly monetary. The truth is that we needed to influence aggregate demand, but in such a way as to create conditions for a recovery of production levels.

Another element which spurred hyperinflation came from the strictly economic sphere: speculation and the public's lack of confidence in the program we were implementing. Because of that, we began to disseminate information massively about the program. The President, in countless meetings with the people, touched on the theme of the economy in order to explain it directly to different social groups. Obviously, it wasn't a plan just directed at attacking demand, but also at bringing about a national *concertación* or consensus.

I never thought it possible to fight hyperinflationary processes with strictly economic elements. It has to be done in a framework of negotiating with all the social sectors of the nation. In that way, what we were trying to do cannot be called an orthodox program. Rather, it was a heterodox program of reform since it emphasized the need for a social and political dialogue in order to bring the nation together around our economic adjustment program.

° *In terms of criticisms of the adjustment program, radical sectors of the left in Nicaragua—both inside and outside of the party—attacked the June 1988 measures and the 1989 program with particular intensity. The magazine Envío attacked the June measures, saying they were "a package without people." Was this policy forced by circumstances or did it reflect an economic doctrine that began when you assumed the economic leadership of the country?*

The economic policy we resorted to was forced on us by circumstances. But the measures we decided on were self-imposed, and weren't imposed by the International Monetary Fund (IMF).

Unfortunately, we had no alternative. Before going ahead with the policy with the vigor with which we did, we sought to convince the National Directorate of its necessity. A long process of discussion took place in which we brought in qualified experts from around the world: Mexicans, Chileans, Spaniards, people from the United States, Soviets, Brazilians, Germans, Czechoslovakians, etc. The adjustment program was discussed and mulled over by countless specialists before the decision was made to go ahead.

There was consensus that we didn't have any alternative to the adjustment. It wasn't a program we designed in order to impose our economic doctrine; instead, it was a practical response to unsustainable macroeconomic imbalances, an economic blockade, and a lack of outside resources. In the end, we resorted to a great domestic sacrifice by utilizing exchange rate, fiscal, and interest rate policies.

Worse, we didn't have enough resources to compensate those sectors adversely affected by the adjustment. But there wasn't a doctrinaire schema behind the adjustment. It's enough to point out that the AFA package[12] of food aid to State employees is far removed from any idea held by the IMF. We maintained subsidies to transportation, electricity, and water even when this contradicted IMF-style logic.

The adjustment program was a pragmatic action decided on by the government economic team; it wasn't drawn up by any one person. Our starting point was to recognize that the crisis demanded we use the instruments of economic policy fully. To have done nothing would have been catastrophic and would have meant a breakup of society.

Unhampered hyperinflation could have led to social chaos with unpredictable consequences. Faced with this eventuality, the government acted with responsibility. And those critics who, like the magazine *Envío,* made the accusation that the June 1988 measures were implemented without taking the people into consideration couldn't offer a better alternative. What we did was the only thing that could be done given the specific conditions of the country.

° *What kind of discussions took place inside the National Directorate and the government about the adjustment program, especially the 1989 measures?*

The hardest discussion was to convince the political leadership of the country that our options were narrowing and that the only thing possible was a radical economic adjustment program.

We had this discussion in December 1988 when the 1989 economic program—which implied a radical reduction in spending for all government sectors, including the armed forces—was presented.

The discussion with the National Directorate went on for almost a month, including Saturdays and Sundays, and we were attempting to convince them that what we should implement weren't measures inspired by a particular economic theory or doctrine, but that they were the only alternative given the hyperinflation that the country was experiencing. I remember that at the beginning, Ortega rejected all the ideas that were put forward.

In the middle of these discussions, I talked at length with the Soviet ambassador to our country and I asked him how they saw the question of aid to Nicaragua in the light of *perestroika*. I explained to him that some saw a need to break with the framework of the mixed economy. The ambassador's reaction was that if, at this time, the Soviet Union had difficulty in helping because of its own problems, it would be even more difficult for them to help if the framework of the mixed economy was broken. His response confirmed for me that we had no alternatives and the arguments in favor of the 1989 program had to be carried to the final consequences.

All these elements, introduced into the discussion in a sweeping way, produced a consensus in 1989 at the level of the National Directorate, although everyone was fully aware of the political costs we would incur.

° *With the implementation of the stabilization program, President Ortega took direct responsibility for the measures being implemented. Elsewhere in the world, it's the ministers of the economy who assume responsibility for economic policy. Wasn't this a political error?*

Ortega was convinced that the program we were going ahead with was the best that we could do. And being convinced of that, it was honest and fair of him to commit himself to it. We hoped he would help regain popular suport for the measures. We were upset that the opposition kept referring to the program as one that had been drawn up outside the country, calling it the "Taylor Plan."

With all due respect to the help we received from North American professor Lance Taylor,[13] the program was drawn up by us. We elaborated our proposals with the opinions of professor Taylor and Dr. Ibarra[14] of the Economic Commission for Latin America (CEPAL).[15] They reaffirmed our ideas, but they didn't change those thoughts.

° *You refer to some specific aspects of the 1989 economic program. What were its goals, and to what degree were they met?*

The 1989 program took the 1988 adjustment further. First, it proposed to fight the hyperinflationary process which had reached dramatic levels in 1988. By the end of 1989, we had gone from 33,000 percent inflation in 1988 to less than 1,700 percent, an effort that was recognized internationally.

The second goal was to bring the level of export earnings back up. And in effect, in 12 months of applying the program, exports increased by almost 30 percent in real terms over the year, a good sign of our capacity to recover our productive abilities.

The very fact that there was a turnaround with exports—above all in non-traditional products—and that imports were reduced showed the benefits of our exchange-rate policy.

Third, we were always concerned in the program to limit the erosion of the purchasing power of the wages of the great majority of Nicaraguan workers. This goal, as shown by the figures, was also met.

Our major goals were met. To have been more successful would have required more international cooperation, which unfortunately didn't come about. To lower the fiscal deficit from 25 percent of the Gross Domestic Product in 1988 to 5 percent in 1989 was an extraordinary feat. With the 1989 adjustment measures, the basis was laid for the beginning of a stage of economic reactivation. Unfortunately, the insufficiency of outside resources didn't allow for a lowering of the social costs of the adjustment. This concern was a central one in the elaboration of the 1990 plan.

° *The stabilization and adjustment program didn't receive financial support from the International Monetary Fund or the World Bank. Nevertheless, the Swedish government gave support by organizing the Conference of Donor Countries in Stockholm. Did that support have political as well as financial ramifications?*

Clearly, we viewed the Conference of Donors as a chance to reconfirm the respect that Nicaragua had won in the international community in the context of open and direct aggression by the United States. The shutting off of resources from the multilateral agencies and U.S. blackmail against other countries imparted a great deal of political value to the Stockholm conference.

Even when we severely lacked resources, we successfully stood up to the actions of the United States and those of the rightist groups in Nicaragua working actively against the conference, actions which overshadowed the process of *concertación*.

° *Are you referring to the meeting held in April 1990 with agricultural producers?*

That was a positive meeting, but one in which the government made concessions and the favored sectors didn't reciprocate.

° *If they were concessions made without reciprocity, then surely that would affect the economic program. Did the credit policy for cotton growers and the payments made to coffee growers increase the deficit and thereby stimulate inflation?*

Yes. That had an important effect, although it was more proof that the economic program wasn't dogmatic, that it could be flexible under certain circumstances. Unfortunately, in this case, negotiation didn't have very encouraging results.

° *Why wasn't there a violent reaction from the workers to the measures adopted as part of this adjustment program and to the accumulated erosion of real wages and living standards over the years? Why didn't popular explosions occur as in Venezuela, Argentina, and Brazil? Why were the workers so docile towards the Sandinista government?*

Demonstrations were held, demands were made, teachers went on strike. We dealt with these problems, but it should be recognized that we didn't go to extremes.

I think that most workers were convinced that even with all the mistakes that we might have made while in government, a class project with a popular content was being promoted. This basically allowed for the political discourse to be accepted by the masses, even when they didn't give it their blessing.

When an adjustment program—applied with the harshness with which we applied it—is carried out by a government which has a basic conflict of interest with the popular sectors, it's a program doomed to failure. I think that's what began to happen after barely 100 days of the new government.

In our case, the cushion wasn't just in having a certain flexibility provided by measures such as the AFA or some subsidies to basic services, but rather that there was the conviction that it was a program needed to favor the majority of the people. Besides, the program was made widely known, it was explained, and there was a vast amount of dissemination of information. The cards were on the table, we were never demagogic, and we never tried to hide the severity of the measures.

Furthermore, it should be recognized that the informal sector also played a cushioning role. It was smart not to hit the informal sector. It provided an appropriate escape valve for the difficult situation that the formal economy was in. An adjustment program can't close off all valves at the same time. That was our experience; it allowed for not shutting off all the valves, and the pressure cooker didn't explode.

The 1990 plan

° *The goals set in the 1989 economic plan, its implementation, and its results appear to have been a success from what you say and according to what the statistics show. How did you expect to continue in 1990? By the end of November 1989, was the 1990 plan ready? What were the main lines of this plan?*

In July 1989, we already had the first draft of the 1990 plan, and for the first time, we planned well in advance. We pushed ourselves in the Secretariat of Planning and Budget (SPP)[16] because the election campaign was coming up and our leaders, in particular Comandante Ortega and *compañero* Sergio Ramírez, were going to be involved. The content of the plan was thoroughly analyzed in the National Planning Council and it was finally approved at the end of November 1989.

We thought an FSLN victory was unquestionable and that most of the adjustment had already been carried out in 1989. The philosophy of the 1990 plan recapitulated the central points and objectives of the 1989 plan but it placed emphasis on a recovery of production levels and living standards and on the restructuring of the State. Partial privatization of some properties was even put forward. The plan contemplated a decided move toward decentralized development and to strengthen the municipalities.

Continuation of an active exchange-rate policy was proposed which would allow for a continued recovery of export levels and would move the country towards having export earnings of close to $1 billion by 1996. We had an optimistic view of the economic future.

We felt that after the elections, new spaces would be opened up with a probable normalization of relations with the United States. We placed a lot of importance on the second Conference of Donors as a forum to continue negotiating bilateral aid for Nicaragua, and we had as a starting point a further reduction of inflation, even though it had been drastically reduced in 1989.

We set ourselves the goal of having an accumulated inflation rate for 1990 that would not exceed 150 percent. The advances made in the peace process would allow for a further reduction in budget allocations for defense and for a redirecting of those resources to the social programs which had been adversely affected in the previous years.

In this way, the 1990 plan lowered the emphasis on the financial-fiscal aspects and placed more importance on raising production and living standards. We set ourselves the goals of further improving real wages, promoting social programs for the most vulnerable sectors, and aggressively training workers and small businesspeople.

° *Two significant reforms were proposed in the 1990 plan: tax reform and decentralization of the banking system. What were the obstacles that the tax structures and the banking system placed in the way of economic life, and how were such reforms viewed?*

The moment had arrived to give more flexibility to the activity of the commercial banks in order to improve their efficiency. The formation of boards of directors with real authority, as well as giving back to the commercial banks their jurisdiction over international operations, seemed to us to be fundamental.

The chain of direct authority of the Central Bank over the rest of the banking system had to be broken, in that way promoting banks which were efficient in receiving and channeling resources for the benefit of society as a whole. In the area of taxation, an integral reform had to be carried out which would allow for the avoidance of double taxation, a reduction of the multiplicity of taxes, and the conferring of progressiveness to the tax system with a greater weight placed on direct taxes. All these were things which the National Planning Council had been wanting for some time.

At the same time in the SPP, with the support of the National Planning Council, we had been working on elaborating a medium- and long-term strategy for the Nicaraguan economy, conscious that economic and political changes in the world and the region were forcing us to lay the basis for confronting the challenges of the next century. This was on our minds: this was the perspective with which we approached 1990.

° *Did the perspective that Sandinismo had of winning the elections and normalizing relations with the United States also include arriving at an understanding with the multilateral agencies such as the World Bank and the IMF?*

In the application of the 1989 program, we were identifying what was important in order to give stability to the adjustment. In that regard, it was necessary to ensure access to international multilateral financing from the Interamerican Development Bank, the Central American Bank, and the World Bank. We even looked optimistically on the possibility of normalizing relations with some countries with which we had debts pending which prevented them from giving financial aid to Nicaragua.

The moment had come to open negotiations with multilateral agencies in order to have access to fresh resources, but we knew this shouldn't be done from the starting point of the classic rules that the IMF had imposed on other countries. Because of that, we felt that the efforts made in 1988 and 1989 were evidence of our track record for the international agencies in terms of showing our ability to determine the program ourselves, control it ourselves, and in that way, prevent pressures from building up that might have affected structural aspects of the revolution.

° *Prior to the February 25 elections, the New York Times and the Washington Post both seemed convinced that the Sandinista Front would win, and they called on the State Department and President George Bush to reach an understanding with Nicaragua and to lift the blockade. What signs did you see of the U.S. government's willingness to change its position towards a Sandinista government which at that time appeared likely to be be elected on February 25?*

The persistent efforts that the Sandinista government made to negotiate with the United States in order to normalize relations, expecially after President Reagan left office, were intensified some months before the elections.

I thought it was possible to normalize relations, and even to lift the embargo, although I thought that this wasn't going to be resolved overnight since there were important forces in the United States which opposed any normalization of relations with Nicaragua.

In this relatively positive panorama, something disconcerting happened which we didn't want to make public. Three days before election day, and after the invasion of Panama, the accounts that the Nicaraguan government had in Panamanian banks were frozen. We were notified by some international banks in Panama that they had received instructions from the Panamanian government to freeze the accounts of the Central Bank of Nicargaua. We protested to the State Department and they refused to accept that the reports were true, but after the evidence was presented to them, they said it had probably been a decision made by the Southern Command of the United States Armed Forces and that the State Department had nothing to with it.

This was a demonstration that, in spite of some positive signs, a great deal of mistrust towards Nicaragua still existed in the United States. They were betting everything on the UNO and, worse, they didn't believe that the Sandinista Front would hand over power in the event that it lost the elections. These actions broke with the logic and content of the talks which had been going on between high-level officials of the Nicaraguan and U.S. governments.

° *In reality, the date of the elections was moved ahead to February 25. According to law, they should have been held towards the end of 1990. I understand that advancing the date created difficulties for the adjustment program, in particular in the fiscal accounts.*

Was it expected that support given by different countries to the electoral process and the commitments made by the United Nations and other multilateral agencies would facilitate the arrival of resources and that the adjustment program wouldn't be affected? What effect did moving the date of the elections up have in terms of spending and in terms of financial discipline?

Moving up the election date was a political decision made by President Ortega in consultation with the National Directorate. There had been commitments made by some Latin American countries to give economic support so that the costs of the electoral process wouldn't have a great deal of effect on the adjustment program. Unfortunately, in practice, the amount of aid was small and the expenses incurred, above all from September 1989 on, were disproportionately large for a country of our size. The Nicaraguan elections cost almost $20 million in a country which had little in the way of foreign exchange from exports. This doesn't even take into account the expenditures made by the political parties.

The electoral process forced an increase in the expenditures that the central government had to make and it placed strains on the adjustment program. This meant that even though we had managed to reduce inflation levels drastically, by the end of 1989 and the beginning of 1990 there was an accumulation of tensions because of an excessive injection of currency back into the economy which reaccelerated the inflationary process.

The last cabinet

° *Let's talk about the change in cabinet that happened in 1988. In April 1988, you were named Minister of Planning. I understand that your new post in the government was in recognition of the fact that as the Minister of Foreign Trade you had defended the need to have a coherent economic policy for so many years and you had criticized the earlier ways of making decisions about the economy. You were given a key responsibility in the implementation of the stabilization and adjustment program in Nicaragua.*

How is it that you won the confidence of the political leadership, and in particular that of Comandante Daniel Ortega, after all the doubts that there had been in the past?

There was implicit recognition of the good work that had been carried out, but I want to make it clear that this wasn't just my work. A great deal of credit goes to the fact that I succeeded in building a good working team with *compañeros* and *compañeras* who had both technical ability and political commitment. They made it possible to carry out the tasks that we set.

But, I also want to make it clear that the National Directorate as such did not mistrust my work, but rather that there had been individual conflicts and divergences in perspective with some members of the National Directorate which I think stemmed largely from mutual ignorance.

For my part, I always had confidence in the National Directorate and I understood the apprehensiveness of some of its members about the technocrat who came in and played an important part in the process of the revolution. Over a long period, I proved myself, just as other *compañeros* proved themselves during extremely difficult times. I didn't give up; I persisted and was absolutely crystal clear about my positions before the eyes of the

National Directorate without compromising my positions and without being opportunistic.

° *Did your obsessiveness in work that I saw in the nine years I worked at your side help any?*

Probably. I wrote countless reports containing my reflections on the economic situation and its influence on the political situation and even on aspects of the defense of the country. I saw my transfer from foreign trade to planning as a clear show of the need that the president and the National Directorate had to give more importance to economic matters. And I dedicated all my efforts to the challenge, always maintaining a critical spirit. That seemed to me to be fundamental in order to advance in the face of the demands that society makes.

° *When the formation of the new cabinet was being discussed and ended with you being named the Minister of Planning, it was rumored that you would be appointed as the President of the Central Bank and that, in reality, economic policy was going to be directed from there. What happened? Why weren't you moved into that post? To what extent was your capacity for leadership of economic policy harmed by being named as head of the Ministry of Planning and not of the Central Bank? Would you have preferred to be the bank president?*

I'll answer those questions frankly. You ask me two years after having been the Minister of Planning and not after having been the President of the Central Bank. The room for action I had in the Ministry of Planning, the more overall perspective I had of the economic, social, and territorial problems, and the possibility I had to present the discussion of economic matters in the National Planning Council in an orderly fashion are things I never would have been able to do in the Central Bank. The advantage that the Ministry of Planning had was not just that it was a ministry, but also that it was a secretariat of the presidency for economic affairs, and that allowed me to see all the angles of economic policy in the government.

When I was asked to transfer to planning, it was after a discussion I had with President Ortega. He told me a reorganization of the State was needed, and although in the beginning it had been thought to move me to the Central Bank, Comandante Ortega believed that I could help him more in the Ministry of Planning.

°   *Do you think the fact that throughout the years of the
    revolutionary government you put forward a particular
    position and didn't adapt it to the political times had an
    influence in receiving this recognition?*

I think it was the coherence of the proposals that I made
throughout all those years that had the most decisive influence. But
in reality, that question should be asked of those who made the
decision to name me to that post.

VI

The Challenges for the Sandinista Opposition

° *The Sandinista's electoral loss places new demands on Sandinismo. What are the main challenges for the FSLN in the 1990's?*

The biggest challenge to the FSLN will be to develop its ideology at the level of the people. I see the 1990's as a crucial stage for the FSLN, and in general for the Latin American left. The spectacular political, technological, and economic changes that happened all over the industrialized planet and in the countries of Eastern Europe in the 1980's represent a reality from which Latin America and Nicaragua cannot hide. In the 1990's, the trend has been to resolve international political conflicts through means other than military force. This is another reality from which Nicaragua cannot escape. Through the 1980's, we maintained the view that the people's project would have to be defended with arms. From that stemmed one of the main efforts of the revolution: consolidation of its military defense. I think the new winds sweeping the world are going to bring us other challenges, especially if peace becomes a reality in this sub-region.

If the United States agrees to drop its militarist views and play a constructive role in the region, our political perspectives will change. In this sense, I think that we as the FSLN are faced with a great dilemma.

    ° *In what way do these challenges seem decisive for Nicaragua?*

The FSLN inherited a power structure focused around three big economic groups and a military force. The revolution tore down those economic groups and built up a new kind of military force, one that brought people together in defense of the revolution. But while we might lessen our focus on military defense, we should not let our attention stray from the economic bases of the revolution.

Now, since the new government came to power in Nicaragua, the three important economic groups are reconstructing themselves: the group led by the Pellas family; the group that the Lacayo family[1] is beginning to control; and another group of young technocrats who were outside of Nicaragua during the revolution and who are grouped around Ernesto Fernández Holmann.

So, the FSLN is responsible for offsetting the weight and influence of these developing economic groups. We need to prepare and push forward a political strategy with the interests of the people at the center that set the country's productive forces into motion for the benefit of the majority and not just one of these ruling groups.

It is necessary to work very seriously on a new conception of development in which justice and equity and firm respect for self-determination would be basic principles, in which the main beneficiary would be society as a whole. The new FSLN we could build through a process of review should be a multi-class party with the ability to undertake civic struggle in the political and social arenas. We should take this project on with a view to being reelected in 1996.

We need a democratic party that practices civic opposition. We should be ready to form alliances with all progressive sectors of the country so long as those alliances reinforce democracy, justice, and respect for national sovereignty.

    ° *You are concerned that we deemphasize the role of military forces in Nicaragua. President Chamorro makes the same appraisal when she points out that if economic development is to occur, a substantial reduction of the country's armed forces is necessary.*

        Can you imagine a Nicaraguan society like that of Costa Rica—in other words, a State without an army?

No, I don't see it that way. A substantial reduction of the armed forces has to be seen within a broader context, one that includes agreements on a regional level. If Central America is demilitarized, and there is no foreign intervention, only *then* could I imagine a Nicaragua without an army. However, as long as the United States considers Central America as its birthright and security zone, we will always need armies in the region. And, of course, there will be one in Nicaragua, too. An accelerated reduction of the armed forces would be a mistake until parallel behavior is demonstrated by the main actor in this confrontation, the United States.

I sincerely believe that if the United States has its *perestroika* —and *if* this includes respect for the rights of peoples to self-determination—I would have no objection to a Central America without armies. So long as that doesn't happen, it's very premature to hope for a complete demilitarization of Nicaragua.

What really interests me is that even as the armed forces are being reduced in size, their role is declining even faster because of the simple fact that civilian affairs have more weight than military affairs. To that degree, economic affairs tend to take on a more decisive role. That's how it's going all over the world, in Eastern Europe, in Western Europe, in Japan.

° *You referred to the strategy of the FSLN towards the new economic groups that are forming. Could you expand on that?*

The FSLN should have the ability to bring together and lead a powerful and multi-faceted economic and social base. This should include workers in the countryside and in the cities who participate actively in running companies and hold shares in them. It would be a Sandinista Front capable of making links with cooperatives and other forms of socialized economy, including small and medium-sized businesses. It would be an FSLN that influences the informal sector, consolidating and organizing it.

In today's world, neo-capitalism can't be confronted with the strategic conceptions that we had in the 1960's and 1970's such as merely having the State control the means of production. That conception failed and is retreating all around the world. Notwithstanding, its failure must not make us submit to neo-liberal projects. Instead, it should make us find our own road to development.

And our own road can be found by taking stock of the past, looking thoroughly at Nicaragua's economy and society as well as the economic and political reality of the world.

° *It's obvious that there are different economic and political projects inside the present government, although none has yet taken shape sufficiently. Some people, of course, say the government should be treated as a bloc and that there is just one capitalist and pro-imperialist project.*

Yet if you explore the contradictions inside the bourgeoisie, theoretical as well as practical differences become obvious.

That's true. The present government doesn't have a uniform consensus of the future they want for this country. There are the young businesspeople who stayed in the country during the revolution who are grouped around Antonio Lacayo.[2] Most of them lived through the experience of the revolution in Nicaragua, and the pragmatism seen in their political activity is fruit of that experience. They have a modernistic, or we could say, a neo-capitalist attitude towards the problems of the country.

There are the big capitalists who were outside Nicaragua for the better part of the 1980's and who are interested in returning to the past. They didn't go through the changes that happened in the country in the last decade.

And then there is an extremely dangerous attitude held by the ultra-right which is represented by Virgilio Godoy, some of the politicians in the UNO, and some sectors of COSEP. They are trying to make a clean slate of the past, wipe out *Sandinismo,* and cancel out the democratic gains.

° *Given these different political stances and economic groups, what future is there for a multi-class Sandinista project?*

If the Sandinista project is understood as democracy, political pluralism, and the participation of the people, then I think that the FSLN has a better future to offer the country—with guarantees of social stability and development—something the present government would have trouble guaranteeing. If the United States carried out a good-neighbor policy, extraordinary possibilities would open up, not just for Nicaragua, but for Central America as a whole.

° *Promoting a mixed economy was always said to be a "pillar" of the revolution. What is your opinion about the generalized policy of State control that was promoted at different times by the Sandinista government during the ten years of revolution? And what is your opinion with respect*

*to the privatization that the new government proposes to
carry out?*

A while ago I asked a friend who has a long revolutionary
experience about the tactical and strategic character of how he
understood the mixed economy of 1980-81. He told me very frankly
that he and a good number of party members saw it as a purely
tactical question and that, in the first years, he longed to reproduce
the Cuban experience.

I told him that in that view lay a big part of our problem: we
were saying one thing and doing another. These inconsistencies
were a dead weight on the workings of the Sandinista government
because while speaking about having a mixed economy, in practice,
we were thinking and acting against it.

Unfortunately, because of these inconsistences and in-
coherencies, there wasn't a serious effort to define what a mixed
economy should be during ten years of government, even though
starting in 1985, Comandante Victor Tirado began to publicly
reaffirm that the mixed economy was a strategic project.

Regarding privatization, it is not a myth or magic formula. I
think there are sectors of the economy where there is room for a
State presence. Our error was, however, to apply a generalized
formula of State control that included restaurants, beauty salons,
vehicle repair shops, etc. That had negative results on efficiency
and discouraged entrepreneurial initiative.

On the other side of the coin, the new government, when it
puts forward the notion of privatization, generalizes it and falls to
the other extreme, one which takes authority and space away from
activities in which the public sector has been and can continue to
be meaningful and efficient for the whole of the national economy.

I think the present government has not been able to distin-
guish between a process of privatization and a plan of simply giving
back to previous owners those properties affected by the revolution.
This confusion is like a tunnel without end. Almost a year has gone
by and they have no coherent privatization program that states
what, how, or when to privatize, and in whose favor it should be
done.

° *So you don't think the process of State control that the
economy went through is irreversible. What then, in your
judgement, are the elements of change introduced by the
revolution that cannot be reversed?*

Something irreversible is the fact that the workers of the countryside and the cities and the people as a whole had the chance to feel that they had their destiny in their own hands, that they were listened to and that they participated in the building of society. Any attempt to try to relegate the workers to a subservient role is going to be very difficult to achieve.

The growing degree of consciousness among workers in the countryside, workers in the cities, and professionals who demand their rights cannot be ignored. With the revolution, people are no longer afraid to organize themselves and gain power. This, in my judgement, is the most important development of these ten years.

In terms of the economy, from my experience as the former Minister of Foreign Trade, I would say that State marketing of basic products had positive results. However, we could have been more flexible so that the producer would have had more space to act autonomously—for example, in obtaining resources from outside the country.

The nationalization of the banks had very positive effects in terms of democratizing credit. However, the extreme centralism in the management of the commercial banks, starting with the Central Bank, resulted in inefficient practices which affected the credit policy and our ability to obtain resources. Decentralization of the Bank, even in the framework of a nationalized financial system, is basic for improving its efficiency.

The changes in the structure of land tenancy as well as the democratization of the health and education systems—although their quality should be improved still—are also important gains worth noting because the reforms in education and healthcare are a *"sine qua non"* for embarking successfully on the road to development. The FSLN should remain vigilant in these areas.

° *You are self-critical about the past and pragmatic with respect to what the new government can do. I have the impression that this stance is not to the liking of some individuals in the Sandinista Front. In fact, the Sandinista ranks are concerned because that kind of pragmatism has allowed for Sandinista technicians to occupy posts in the present government.*

No one can say for sure what the Sandinista ranks are thinking so long as the party doesn't have a real democratic process of discussion and consultation.

The criticisms made about Sandinista *compañeros* who are in the State apparatus are off the mark. Those kinds of judgements just don't take into account the great transformations that have happened in the country and that make it possible, as in all democracies, for a change in government to *not* automatically result in a massive exodus of technicians and professionals.

That radicalism stems from an all-or-nothing conception held by some *compañeros* of the Sandinista Front who do not separate the roles of the State, the government, the party, the mass organizations, and the rest of society. The bureaucracy of a democratic country which aspires to a modernization of the State should be a stable structure so that changes in governments don't bring about traumatic ruptures. We need to understand that in a democratic society, the State is not the birthright of any one political party, even when the government is led by a given party. Moreover, no one has the right to demand that Sandinista workers enter the ranks of the unemployed because their party lost the elections, or that UNO supporters should if they were to lose the next ones.

In Nicaragua, we lost the elections in a democratic process. The work of public-sector functionaries, besides being a necessity, is fundamental for the survival of the State, regardless of the government.

° *You point out that it is necessary to change a certain mindset of some FSLN members so that they adapt themselves to the new times. But isn't it also necessary to change the extremely centralized structure of the FSLN?*

I would say that there are many of us in the FSLN who see the need for change. We think that *Sandinismo* either must change or history will sweep it away. Conceptions and styles of work must be changed. Ideologized schemes have to be abandoned, and likewise, the top-down, verticalist structures—which had a place in our history when we needed to exert political and military force— have to go, too.

The Sandinista Front is endowed with a great deal of human capability; it has leaders with ample experience and ability. The challenge is to find the appropriate mechanisms so that consensus is reached and so that the diverse opinions are channeled in a democratic way. In any case, coming into the 21st century, it seems to me that extreme positions and verticalist schemes have no future inside *Sandinismo.*

° *Let's talk about the future. Is Sandinismo willing to wait patiently for six years until the next elections? Is it willing to participate politically in the democratic bodies that have been created in the country, discussing things in the National Assembly, in the pertinent organizations of civilian society, and in the press? Is Sandinismo prepared for a democratic political struggle?*

I don't want to get ahead of what will be the final position that the Sandinista Front will adopt. In the near future, a congress will discuss a more concrete definition of what the role of the party will be in the country's new political situation. I can't speak for all Sandinistas, but I can speak about my view on this theme. The world today has changed, and it has changed in some ways in favor of democratic forces. The Sandinista Front, in my opinion, should aspire to have full political participation in all the forums that there are in the country and, over the next six years, it should work within the system to win the next elections.

Our role should be to work hard, efficiently, and responsibly, to be a constructive opposition in the institutions that the revolution itself created and which are also embodied in the Constitution.

We need to comprise a constructive opposition to the UNO government—on the basis of the unyielding defense of popular interests—which would help overcome the economic breakdown resulting from years of aggression. We should push ahead with a real attempt to negotiate and bring efforts together in order to get the country moving on the basis of a minimum consensus.

This view, in my opinion, is the one that the Sandinista Front should hold. I think we should seek a broad national consensus with all sectors willing to make a contribution to economic development and the deepening of democracy in Nicaragua.

In Nicaragua, in the decade of the 1990's, we need a constructive left, not a left of confrontation, if we are to work in favor of *concertación* and consensus. It is necessary that the FSLN participate with the idea of setting things in motion within the climate of peace that has been created in the country and with respect for the institutions that we ourselves created.

If the Sandinista Front doesn't fully respect the society that we created, then we'll be on the road to the status of a mini-party. People aren't waiting for the Sandinista Front to make the rallying call that presents only one option, the option of war; instead, it has to be a Sandinista Front that raises the banner of peace and that, in addition, promotes economic development with social justice, equity, and national independence.

The Sandinista Front should play an active role in the Socialist International.[3] The FSLN should participate actively to help broaden the participation of the left within that organization. The FSLN has made profound contributions to the history of Nicaragua and Latin America. This important experience is an undeniable contribution to revolutionary movements around the world and it should be shared.

° *Let's imagine that there is a new Sandinista government six years hence. What would you do as the minister responsible for economic policy?*

That depends on what conditions the government is received in then. I sincerely hope that in 1996, a basis for economic stability will have been established. It's difficult for me to predict now how Nicaragua will be in 1996, but anyway, there has to be a rehabilitation of industry here, and if this government doesn't do it, then it will fall on us to do it. Only in that way can we insert ourselves in a more dynamic way into world trade.

There have to be advances made in recovering our export capacity, and if this doesn't happen in the coming years, I think the outcome will be disastrous. The population is growing at an annual rate of 3 percent and that means that the pie has to grow more rapidly than that in order to assure a minimum slice to this growing population.

I hope I don't find myself thinking about emphasizing the need to reduce the fiscal deficit or about the exchange-rate policy that we are going to follow. Instead, I would rather see myself putting more emphasis on the question of how to assure that there is dynamic expansion of agriculture and industrial development that would bring the growing mass of Nicaraguans into active employment.

I would rather see myself thinking about the development of an efficient and competitive Nicaragua; thinking about training workers and small businesspeople; thinking about improving primary, secondary, and university education; thinking about what initiatives to take in order to preserve the environment and to safeguard a healthy life for this growing population.

To conclude, I think it is becoming more evident that the economic viability of small countries like those of Central America is being put into question. Because of this, I see that if the FSLN becomes the government again in 1996, the party and Nicaragua should push vigorously for joint Central American efforts in the areas of research and development and in regards to education and health programs with a more regional focus. The establishment of a confederation of Central American states is a dream worth keeping alive.

I visualize a Nicaragua with great potential, which we will achieve only with a national concerted effort. By respecting the changes that have taken place in the country's social and economic structures, we might enter into a phase of greater efficiency and productivity. Nicaragua could become an international model in our management of economics, society, politics, and morality.

Notes

Chapter I

1. Violeta Barrios de Chamorro. Widow of Dr. Pedro Joaquín Chamorro. Owner of the daily newspaper *La Prensa*. In 1979, she was invited to be part of the first Government Junta after the overthrow of the Somoza dictatorship. She resigned in 1980. In 1989, the 14-party coalition UNO nominated her as its presidential candidate for the February 25, 1990 elections. She belongs to no political party and she won the presidential election with 54 percent of the vote.

2. UNO—National Opposition Union. This Nicaraguan political coalition brings together 12 parties and two party factions which do not have legal recognition. In it, among others, are three Liberal parties, two Conservative parties, three Social Christian (or Christian Democratic) parties, three Social Democratic parties, and one Marxist party.

3. Dr. Francisco Mayorga. President of the Central Bank of Nicaragua from April 25 to October 31, 1990. A professor at the Central American Institute of Business Administration (INCAE) until 1989. During the first years of Sandinista rule, he was Nicaragua's representative to the Central American Bank of Economic Integration (BCIE). He is not a member of any party.

4. United Nations Development Program—UNDP. An international agency which has maintained a program of technical cooperation with Nicaragua since 1979.

5. Sergio Ramírez Mercado. Lawyer and novelist, a renowned Latin American political and literary figure. Member of the Group of Twelve during the insurrection in 1978 and 1979 and member of the Government Junta of National Reconstruction from 1979 until 1984 when he was elected Vice-president of the Republic. FSLN Vice-presidential candidate in 1990. Currently, he is head of the Sandinista bench in the National Assembly. He is a member of the FSLN and a member of the Sandinista Assembly.

6. First Conference of Donors in Stockholm. A meeting of donor countries to respond to the efforts at economic stabilization that the Sandinista government was making in 1989. Held in Stockholm,

Sweden in May 1989 under the auspices of the Swedish government.

7. Transition Accords. The transition from the former president to the president-elect necessitated a process of high-level talks in which the basis was worked out so that a peaceful transition from one government to the next would occur. The commitment was made to respect the constitutional infrastructure created in the past ten years. Furthermore, it was guaranteed that there would be a climate of security and tranquility for the whole Nicaraguan family. These accords were contained in an historic document signed between the outgoing government and the government-elect on March 27, 1990.

8. Albert Fishlow. Professor of Economics at the University of California, Berkeley. Professor Fishlow is an expert on development and economic stabilization. He was chosen by the countries that participated in the Stockholm Conference to preside over the Commission of Follow-up to the 1989 Nicaraguan Economic Program which regularly produced reports about the execution of the Sandinista government's stabilization program. Fishlow is a member of the Consultative Council of the International Foundation for the Global Economic Challenge (FIDEG).

9. Virgilio Godoy Reyes. Lawyer. After the 1979 triumph, he was Minister of Labor until 1984 when he resigned. He was president of the Independent Liberal Party (PLI) until October 1990. He was nominated by the UNO to be its Vice-presidential candidate in the 1990 elections. He was elected along with Violeta Chamorro.

10. COSEP—Superior Council of Private Enterprise. Groups together private business organizations of the country.

11. Pedro Joaquín Chamorro Cardenal. Lawyer and director of the daily newspaper *La Prensa* until his death in 1978. An outstanding political figure who fought against the Somoza dictatorship, a fight which led him to be jailed, tortured, and finally assassinated in January 1978. His death provoked a popular uprising which contributed to the defeat of the Somoza family dictatorship. He was an untiring fighter for free expression, free thought, and national independence.

12. Robelo group. The *contra* faction led by Alfonso Robelo, an engineer who had been a part of the Government Junta of National

Reconstruction. Robelo joined the counterrevolutionaries, then later resigned to focus on his private enterprise.

13. Humberto Ortega Saavedra. Member of the FSLN National Directorate since the early 1970's. He led the *tercerista* faction together with his brother Daniel and Victor Tirado. An outstanding Latin American political and military strategist. Minister of Defense for ten years of the revolution and chief of the armed forces since 1979. After the electoral victory of Violeta Chamorro, she asked him to stay on as Commander-in-Chief of the Nicaraguan army. Because of this, he was obliged to resign from his honorific post as a member of the FSLN leadership in order to respect the principle of having an apolitical armed forces.

Chapter II

1. Carlos Fonseca. Comandante-in-Chief of the Sandinista Peoples' Revolution. Founder of the FSLN. From an early age, he denounced the Somoza dictatorship and formed different political-military movements. He drafted the FSLN Historical Program and gave it its stamp of nationalism, adopting the figure of General Augusto César Sandino as the best one to gather together the aspirations for the construction of a new society with social justice and respect for the self-determination of the Nicaraguan nation. He died in combat against Somoza's National Guard in 1977.

2. *Tercerista* faction. In the 1970's, the FSLN divided into three different factions based on different forms of struggle against the Somoza dictatorship. There was the Prolonged People's War (GPP) faction whose official representatives to the unification of the FSLN were Tomás Borge, Henry Ruiz, and Bayardo Arce. The Proletarian faction was led by Jaime Wheelock, Luis Carrión, and Carlos Núñez. The *tercerista* or Insurrectional faction was led by Daniel Ortega, Humberto Ortega, and Victor Tirado. This faction called on broad sectors of Nicaraguan society to participate in the pre-insurrectional struggle. This work resulted in the formation of the Group of Twelve. It launched the final offensive that brought the 1979 triumph, but not before the three factions had united to form one National Directorate.

3. Daniel Ortega Saavedra. Member of the FSLN National Directorate since the 1970's. Outstanding national and international political figure. Member of the Government Junta of National

Reconstruction from 1979 to 1984 when he was elected President for the 1984-1990 period as the FSLN candidate. Ortega was the FSLN presidential candidate in the 1990 elections. In 1984, as well as being President, he was the Coordinator of the Political Commission of the National Directorate. Since a very early age, his life was one of rebellion, prudence, and moral strength. He suffered seven years of imprisonment and torture in the fight against the Somoza dictatorship.

4. Victor Tirado López. Member of the FSLN National Directorate since the early 1970's. He led, together with the Ortega brothers, the *tercerista* faction before the 1979 triumph. For 10 years of Sandinista government, he handled the party's relations with mass organizations, particularly the campesino and worker sectors. He has never held a governmental post.

5. Ernesto "Tito" Castillo Martínez. A lawyer who was part of the Group of Twelve before the 1979 insurrection. An academic and a fighter against Somoza. Member of the Sandinista Assembly. After the revolutionary triumph, he held the post of Attorney General and later became the Minister of Justice before being named as Nicaragua's ambassador to the U.S.S.R. until April 25, 1990.

6. Alfredo César. Engineer. Linked to the capital of the Pellas family. Worked in the San Antonio sugar refinery before 1979. Joined the FSLN in 1978 and was the secretary to the Government Junta of National Reconstruction after the 1979 triumph. Later, he held the post of Minister of the International Fund for Reconstruction (FIR). He participated in the negotiations over Nicaragua's foreign debt to international banks when he was president of the Central Bank, a post he occupied until 1982. He quit *Sandinismo* and joined the counterrevolution with Edén Pastora in the Southern Opposition Bloc (BOS), becoming one of the main leaders of what came to be called the Nicaraguan Resistance. Currently, he is the first secretary of the executive in the National Assembly. He belongs to the Social Democratic Party. He returned to Nicaragua under the 1988 amnesty decreed by the Sandinista government. He is the brother-in-law of Antonio Lacayo, the Minister of the Presidency in Violeta Chamorro's cabinet.

7. Reynaldo Antonio Téfel. Founder of the Institute for Human Promotion (INPRHU) prior to the revolutionary triumph. He joined the Group of Twelve before the final insurrection of 1979. He was the Minister of Social Welfare until April 1990. Currently, he is an

FSLN deputy and a member of the executive of the National Assembly.

8. Carlos Tünnermann. Rector of the National Autonomous University of Nicaragua (UNAN) before the 1979 triumph. He was a member of the Group of Twelve. After July 1979, he was the Minister of Education and made an important contribution in the execution of the National Literacy Crusade. After that, he was named Nicaraguan ambassador in Washington. He was a member of the Sandinista bench in the National Assembly from 1984 to 1990. Currently, he is a member of the UNESCO council.

9. Roberto Mayorga. Economist. After the 1979 triumph, he was the Minister of Planning until early 1980. He was the representative of the Sandinista government in different international economic forums before withdrawing his services from the government in 1984. Afterwards, he worked as a private consultant in Washington, and after the election victory of Violeta Chamorro, he became Nicaraguan ambassador to the United Nations.

10. Joaquín Cuadra Chamorro. Outstanding Nicaraguan jurist of international renown who joined the Group of Twelve before the revolutionary triumph. He is the father of Major-General Joaquín Cuadra Lacayo, the head of the chiefs-of-staff of the Sandinista People's Army (EPS). He was named as the Finance Minister in the Sandinista government in July 1979 and was the chief negotiator of the foreign debt with the international banks. During the ten years of Sandinista government, he was Nicaragua's representative to the International Monetary Fund, the World Bank, and the Interamerican Development Bank. He held the post of minister-president of the Central Bank of Nicaragua from 1984 until April 1990.

11. Rogelio Ramírez Mercado. Sociologist and lawyer. Former Minister of Municipal Services. Former Nicaraguan ambassador to Costa Rica and other Central American countries for the Sandinista government. Sandinista deputy in 1984. Currently, he is a member of the Sandinista bench in the National Assembly.

12. Agustín Lara. Member of the FSLN. Member of the Sandinista Assembly and political secretary of the FSLN in Region V (Boaco, Chontales). Ministerial Delegate of the Presidency in different regions of the country. Currently, he is the director of Radio Sandino.

13. Alfonso Robelo. Engineer. Majority stockholder in the Greases and Oils Company (GRACSA). President of the Association of Private Businessmen in the Nicaraguan Development Institute (INDE) before 1979. He was a founder of the Nicaraguan Democratic Movement (MDN) which operated in the country during the anti-Somoza struggle. He was part of the first Government Junta of National Reconstruction from which he resigned some months later. He left Nicaragua a few months after that and joined the counterrevolutionary movement and reached the position of being one of its leaders. He later resigned and dedicated himself to his private businesses. After the electoral victory of Violeta Chamorro, he was named Nicaraguan ambassador to Costa Rica.

14. Jaime Wheelock Román. Comandante of the Revolution and member of the FSLN National Directorate. Before the reunification of the FSLN, he was one of the leaders of the Proletarian faction. He is the author of a number of books. After the revolutionary triumph in 1979, he became the Minister of Agrarian Reform and Agricultural Development (MIDINRA), a post he occupied until April 25, 1990. Inside the National Directorate, he is a member of the Political Commission.

15. Tomás Borge Martínez. Comandante of the Revolution, member of the FSLN National Directorate, and poet. He is the only survivor of the three original founders of the Sandinista Front for National Liberation. Before the FSLN reunited, he was a leader of the Prolonged People's War (GPP) faction. In the fight against Somoza, he was jailed and brutally tortured. After the 1979 Sandinista triumph, he was a member of the collective leadership body of the FSLN, and was the Minister of the Interior until April 1990. He is the author of a number of books which have been published in several different languages.

16. René Núñez Téllez. Renowned Sandinista and anti-Somoza fighter. Since the reunification of the FSLN, he has been the secretary to the National Directorate. In 1984, as well as holding the post mentioned above, he was named as the Minister of the Presidency, a position he held until April 25, 1990. Within the National Directorate, he was in charge of relations between the party, the government, and the Catholic Church. He is a member of the Sandinista Assembly.

17. Henry Ruiz Hernández ("Modesto"). Comandante of the Revolution and member of the FSLN National Directorate. Together with

Tomás Borge and Bayardo Arce, he led the GPP faction of the FSLN before the reunification. From 1980 to 1984, he was the Minister of Planning. In 1984, he became the Minister of Foreign Cooperation. Since April 1990, he has had the responsiblity for handling the FSLN's foreign affairs.

18. Edmundo Jarquín. Lawyer. During the anti-Somoza struggle, he was a close collaborator of Pedro Joaquín Chamorro with whom he organized a student movement known as the Democratic Liberation Union (UDEL). He was the Minister of the International Fund for Reconstruction (FIR) in the first years of the revolution. Later, he was named Nicaraguan ambassador to Mexico and Spain. In the February 1990 elections, he was elected as a deputy for the FSLN. Currently, he is the second secretary to the executive of the National Assembly.

19. Rodrigo Carazo Odio. President of Costa Rica during the period of the 1979 insurrectional war in Nicaragua. After he left the presidency, he organized the University of Peace and continues to work there.

20. Somoza. The family that governed Nicaragua for almost 50 years. The founder of the dynasty, Anastasio Somoza García, was put in place by the U.S. occupation force during the 1936 intervention. Somoza García was assassinated in 1954 and his son Luís was in power until he died of a heart attack. His younger brother, Anastasio, the chief of the National Guard, then took power. Anastasio Somoza Debayle was overthrown by the FSLN-led insurrection in July 1979 after a bloody civil war which claimed 50,000 victims and in which the National Guard bombed the civilian population in more than five cities of the country. The Somoza family owned a great deal of productive land as well as countless companies that operated in different branches of the national economy. Theft, torture, and death were constants of the behavior of this dictatorship.

21. Policarpo Paz García. President of the Republic of Honduras and a retired general of the Honduran Armed Forces. He was President during the insurrectional struggle in Nicaragua.

22. William Bowdler. Ambassador-at-large and special envoy of U.S. President Jimmy Carter. In 1979, he acted as the White House emissary in order to find a way to remove Somoza and contain the coming FSLN triumph.

23. Dionisio "Nicho" Marenco. Engineer and business administrator. Student leader at his university. He worked for some time at the San Antonio sugar refinery. Member of the Sandinista Assembly. After the revolutionary triumph, he was the Minister of Construction and Transport. In 1982, he was the Minister of Domestic Commerce and, in 1985, the Minister of Planning. Since 1988, he has been the director of the FSLN Agitation and Propaganda Office (DAP) and played an important role in the 1990 election campaign.

24. National Guard. The name that the Somoza dictatorship gave to the army which repressed the people for more than 50 years.

25. Institute of Foreign and Domestic Trade—INCEI. The governmental entity during the Somoza reign in charge of regulating the prices of basic grains in the national market. It was dissolved by the Sandinista government, and the System of Foreign and Domestic Commerce was set up in its place. This system was organized with the creation of the Ministry of Foreign and Domestic Trade in August 1979. INCEI, as such, was replaced by the National Company for the Supply of Basic Foodstuffs (ENABAS).

26. Emilio Baltodano Cantarero. Member of the FSLN. Member of the Sandinista Assembly. Secretary to the Government Junta of National Reconstruction where he played an important role. After that, he was the Minister of Industry until 1988, and then he was the Vice-minister of Agricultural Development and presided over the boards of directors of the State-run agricultural corporations until 1990.

27. William Hüpper Argüello. Economist. FSLN member. Vice-minister of Finance from the beginning of the revolutionary triumph. From 1985 to April 25, 1990, he was the Finance Minister.

28. Alfredo Alaniz Downing. Economist. Member of the FSLN. President of the Central Bank of Nicaragua in 1981. He was Minister of the Nicaraguan Institute of Fisheries (INPESCA), Nicaraguan ambassador to the People's Republic of China, and later, the ambassador to the Republic of the United Mexican States until April 25, 1990.

29. Félix Contreras. Economist. Member of the FSLN. He held different posts since 1979 in the Ministry of Planning and, later, in the Ministry of Foreign Cooperation.

30. Orlando Núñez. Sociologist. Member of the FSLN. Founder and director of the Center for Economic Investigations of the Agrarian Reform (CIERA).

31. Alvaro Guzmán Cuadra. Foreign Trade Vice-minister from 1979 to 1982. Minister of the Nicaraguan Mining Institute (INMINE). Chief of the penitentiary system within the Ministry of the Interior until 1989. After that, he held the post of second-in-command of the Sandinista Police.

32. Standard Fruit Company. U.S. banana company which began operations in Nicaragua in 1964. It rented lands and produced and traded bananas. It pulled out in 1981.

33. José Antonio Baltodano. Businessperson. He has held the post of executive director of ENCAFE since its creation.

34. ENCAFE—Nicaraguan Coffee Company. Company ascribed to the Ministry of Foreign Trade. In charge of buying coffee nationally and selling it on the international market.

35. Enrique Pereira. Engineer. Partner in the Solórzano, Villa, and Pereira (SOVIPE) construction firm. During the period of the Somoza government, it developed residential projects and financial companies (Real Estate Company for Savings and Loans, Ltd.)

36. Alfredo and Nicolás Marín. Brothers who were part of the Fernández Holmann group before the 1979 triumph. Both are businesspeople, and Nicolás has also been a professor of finance at the Central American Business Administration Institute (INCAE).

37. Ernesto Fernández Holmann. Economist. Executive president of the Bank of America until the revolutionary triumph. Capitalist linked to the Pellas family's capital. Fernández Holmann left Nicaragua before the triumph and founded an international bank in Grand Cayman Island through which, it is speculated, the major part of the capital that left Nicaragua from 1977 to 1979 flowed. He was president of the People's Bank in Miami.

38. Pellas group. Under this name is included the Chamorro family of Granada, Benard, and Solórzano, among others. It brings together the biggest capital in Nicaragua and has business operations in sugar cane (with the San Antonio sugar refinery), Flor de Caña rums, and Toña breweries. In addition, it is the Toyota distributor and has a soap factory and a concentrates factory, among other

holdings. Pellas had its greatest expression in the Bank of America which was nationalized after the revolutionary triumph.

39. Mario Hannon. Agricultural producer and businessperson who stayed in Nicaragua throughout the entire revolutionary period. His main activity is rice production.

40. Samuel Mancel. Agricultural producer and businessperson who, like Mr. Hannon, remained in the country during the ten years of the revolution. His main activity is also rice production.

41. Enrique Dreyfuss. Engineer. At the time of the triumph of the Sandinista People's Revolution, he was president of the Nicaraguan Chamber of Industries (CADIN). In 1980, he was president of COSEP. He remained in Nicaragua during the whole decade of the 1980's, in charge of the industrial company CERISA. He was a founder of the Commission for the Recovery and Development of Nicaragua (CORDENIC) and its president. He is a member of the Sanford Commission and is now Nicaragua's Foreign Minister.

42. Arturo Cruz. Economist. Retired official of the Interamerican Development Bank. He joined the Group of Twelve before the insurrection. After the triumph, he held the post of president of the Central Bank of Nicaragua. After Alfonso Robelo resigned, he was asked to join the Government Junta of National Reconstruction. He was Nicaraguan ambassador in Washington. He resigned from that post and joined the executive body of the armed counterrevolution. In 1984, he quit that and returned to Nicaragua in order to run as the presidential candidate in the 1984 elections. While in Nicaragua and running for the opposition, he quit before the election date and returned to the United States in order to go into academic life.

43. In reference to a quote from General Augusto César Sandino in regards to his struggle against the U.S. occupation of Nicaragua in the 1920's and early 1930's: "Only the workers and campesinos will go all the way."

Chapter III

1. Contadora Group. Latin American group created in 1985 in order to find a negotiated solution to the conflicts in the Central American region. The Contadora Group was made up of representatives from

Mexico, Panama, Venezuela, Brazil, and Argentina. Later, Colombia, Peru, and Ecuador joined.

2. Esquipulas. Refers to the Central American presidential summit meeting at which, in 1987, agreements were signed to find a peaceful solution to the regional conflicts.

3. Pochomil. A Nicaraguan beach resort 50 kilometers from Managua.

4. FMLN. The Salvadoran revolutionary movement known as the Farabundo Martí Front for National Liberation.

5. Orlando Solórzano. Economist. Specialist in themes of industrial development and regional integration. Before the revolutionary triumph, he had been an advisor to the Nicaraguan Chamber of Industry and an international officer of the Secretariat for Central American Economic Integration (SIECA). After the 1979 triumph, he was the Vice-minister of Foreign Trade and later of Planning until April 1990. He was responsible for handling relations with the other countries of Central America.

6. *Buhoneros.* Known in Nicaragua as informal merchants who buy and sell products in the Central American area using barter mechanisms.

7. La Concha. A town in Nicaragua around which a large part of the Nicaraguan pineapple production is cultivated. It is located only a few kilometers from the city of Masaya.

8. Reginaldo Panting. Minister of Economy of the Republic of Honduras during the term of President José Azcona.

9. Sébaco Valley. A fertile valley in the Matagalpa region where an agro-industrial complex has been developed.

10. Front men. Those who lend their name to a contract in order to hide the identity of the real owner.

11. Office of the Attorney General *(Procurada de la Justicia).* Entity created after the 1979 revolutionary triumph. Legally represents the State of Nicaragua.

12. Clearing House. The regional entity of the Central American Monetary Council in which the payments among the Central Banks of the Central American countries are liquidated.

13. GATT—General Agreement on Tariffs and Trade. Multilateral organization created to regulate international trade. Nicaragua was an initial signatory of that agreement in 1950.

Chapter IV

1. Central American Common Market. Created at the beginning of the 1960's after the signing of a general treaty to which the five countries of the Central American region adhere.

2. Ministry of Foreign Cooperation. Entity of the Nicaraguan government created in 1984 as a substitute for the International Fund for Reconstruction (FIR). It had the function of handling international relations in regards to bilateral aid to Nicaragua.

3. Haroldo Montealegre. Financier. After the triumph of the revolution, he was named the Vice-minister of the Economy and the Minister of the FIR. He resigned in 1982 and stayed outside the country until returning after the February 1990 elections. He has been named by President Chamorro as the minister in charge of negotiating Nicaragua's foreign debt.

4. Comptroller General of the Republic. Entity created after the revolutionary triumph as a substitute for the Tribunal of the Republic's Accounts. Its main function was to control governmental administration. It is directed by Emilio Baltodano Pallais, who has held the post through the entire revolutionary period until the present.

5. Valpy Fitzgerald. Professor at Cambridge University, England and at the Institute of Social Studies in the Hague. He has been an advisor to a number of Latin American governments.

6. Francisco "Che" Lainez. Economist. Founder and first president of the Central Bank of Nicaragua in the early 1960's. He later resigned from the government and was named as an advisor to the movement that Dr. Pedro Joaquín Chamorro organized.

7. Roberto Incer Barquero. Economist. President of the Central Bank of Nicaragua in the last years of the government of Anastasio Somoza Debayle. After 1979, he joined the technical team of the International Monetary Fund in Washington, D.C., where he continues to work.

8. Ministry of Planning—MIPLAN. Created after the triumph of the revolution. Its first minister was Dr. Roberto Mayorga.

9. National Planning Council—CNP. A presidential body created to coordinate the Sandinista government's economic policy. Participating in it were the Vice-president of the Republic; the Minister of Foreign Cooperation; the Minister of Agricultural Development; the Minister of Economy, Industry, and Commerce; the Minister of Finance; the Central Bank; and the head of the Secretariat of Planning and Budget, the entity which acted as secretary to the CNP presided over by the President.

10. Area of People's Property—APP. The State-owned property in the companies affected by decrees of the revolutionary government in the agricultural, industrial, and service sectors. It symbolized the access of the people to economic power.

11. Political Commission of the National Directorate. Internal body of the National Directorate coordinated by Daniel Ortega.

12. Ministerial delegates of the president. From 1984 on, after the country was divided into regions, the President of the Republic named presidential representatives to each region of the country. Besides having ministerial responsibilities, the people named were usually the political secretaries of the Sandinista Front in their regions.

Chapter V

1. Roberto Gutiérrez Huelva. Civil engineer. Member of the FSLN. Vice-minister of Agricultural Development since the 1979 triumph. In 1985, he was named as first vice-president of the Central Bank of Nicaragua, a post he held until April 25, 1990.

2. Ramón Cabrales. Guerrilla Comandante. Director-general of Customs after the 1979 triumph. Ministerial delegate of the Presidency of the Republic to Region IV (Granada, Carazo, Rivas). Minister of Domestic Commerce and, later, Vice-minister of Economy, Industry, and Commerce until April 25, 1990.

3. Néstor Avedaño. Economist. Vice-minister of Planning after the triumph of the revolution. Later, he was named as the director of the National Nutrition Program (PAN). Secretary-General of the Ministry of Foreign Cooperation until April 25, 1990.

4. Xavier Gorostiaga. Jesuit priest. Economist. Founder and president of CRIES (Regional Coordinator of Economic and Social Investigations). After the revolutionary triumph, he was an advisor to the Ministry of Planning.

5. Alban Lataste. Economist. International advisor from the United Nations Development Program to the Ministry of Planning.

6. Plan Bertha. Name given to the operation of preparing the new currency. The new bills were printed in the German Democratic Republic.

7. Olof Palme Convention Center. Constructed in the memory of the late Swedish Prime Minister, Olof Palme. It is located in the center of Managua, the capital of Nicaragua.

8. National Literacy Crusade. Also known as the Peoples' Literacy Crusade. Carried out just months after the revolutionary triumph. It allowed for a reduction in the illiteracy rate to less than 20 percent of the total population.

9. Popular Health Campaigns. Refers to the campaigns which counted on the participation of the people to vaccinate children and prevent diseases.

10. National System of Organization of Labor and Salaries—SNOTS. It set occupational ranges in order to determine salaries on a national level. This system was abolished in 1988.

11. Hurricane Joan. Swept through Nicaragua in October 1988, entering from the Atlantic side. It crossed the country in a way never before seen and left for the Pacific. The damages it caused to the national economy were estimated at $840 million by the Economic Commission for Latin America (CEPAL) of the United Nations.

12. AFA. Spanish acronym for rice, beans, and sugar (arroz, frijoles, azucar). A program to guarantee food supplies, begun in 1988, which covered public sector workers and those working in State-owned companies. These products were provided to workers on a monthly basis at highly subsidized prices.

13. Lance Taylor. Outstanding international economist born in the United States. Expert in development and structural adjustment. Professor at the Massachusetts Institute of Technology (MIT). Contracted by the Swedish Agency for International Development in

order to head up an advisory group formed in 1989 to follow the adjustment program of the Nicaraguan government. Professor Taylor is on the Consultative Council of the International Foundation for the Global Economic Challenge (FIDEG).

14. David Ibarra. Economist. Advisor to CEPAL and former Minister of the Treasury Department of the Mexican government. On countless occasions, the Nicaraguan government requested Dr. Ibarra's services as an advisor in the economic field.

15. CEPAL—Economic Commission for Latin America. A body of the United Nations that carries out economic studies in the Latin American region.

16. Secretariat of Planning and Budget—SPP. Name given to the new Ministry of Planning after 1984, charged with preparing the economic policy proposals that were presented to the National Planning Council.

Chapter VI

1. Lacayo family. Refers to the group made up of the two brothers César and Carlos Reynaldo, heirs to the import-export firm OCAL. Their economic power grew during the time of the Sandinista government. Currently, the group continues to grow, organizing strong networks of influence in all levels of the government structure. Distant family relation to the Minister of the Presidency.

2. Antonio Lacayo Oyanguren. Engineer. Businessperson and partner of Alfonso Robelo in the Greases and Oils Company (GRACSA). Lacayo was part of CORDENIC (Commission for the Recovery and Development of Nicaragua), an organization of young businesspeople who believe in the modernization of capital. CORDENIC counterpoised itself to the more conservative ideas of the politicized association, COSEP. He was named as campaign manager of the UNO for the 1990 presidential elections. After the February 25, 1990 elections, Violeta Chamorro named him the Minister of the Presidency. He has played an outstanding role in negotiating and ratifying the Transition Agreements on behalf of the government. The son-in-law of President Chamorro, he is considered to be the strongest person in the new government.

3. Socialist International. International organization which brings together many parties of the European center-left as well as Social Democratic parties in Latin America and other regions of the world. Among many outstanding figures that have been in the Socialist International are Willy Brandt and Olof Palme.

Chronology

Chronology of Relevant Political and Economic Events

1977

JULY

The dictator Somoza suffers a heart attack and the process of capital flight from Nicaragua begins.

SEPTEMBER

The Group of Twelve is formed due to the initiative taken by the *tercerista* faction of the FSLN.

1978

JANUARY

10 - Pedro Joaquín Chamorro is assassinated.

21 - COSEP calls for a business strike to protest the assassination and is supported by the Democratic Liberation Union (UDEL).

28 - Demonstrations break out in all the cities. Somoza declares a State of Emergency.

FEBRUARY

1 and 2 - The *tercerista* faction of the FSLN attacks the National Guard garrisons in Rivas and Granada and withdraws to Costa Rica.

20 - The people of the Monimbó neighborhood of Masaya rise up against an act of repression committed by the National Guard.

MARCH

1 - Business groups reluctant to join the UDEL because they consider that there is too much of a leftist presence in it found the Nicaraguan Democratic Movement (MDN) led by Alfonso Robelo.

25 - The Association of Workers of the Countryside (ATC) is formed in Diriamba.

APRIL

6 - The Venezuelan government asks the Organization of American States (OAS) to investigate human rights violations in Nicaragua.

JUNE

1 - In the manifesto of its Great Convention in Monimbó, the Independent Liberal Party (PLI) condemns all attempts to hold a dialogue with Somoza and recognizes the FSLN as the vanguard of the peoples' revolutionary rebellion because of its democratic mystique, its discipline, and the courage shown in its struggles.

16 - In New York, Somoza announces that he won't leave the government before 1981.

28 - The Group of Twelve announces that its members will return to Nicaragua on July 5, 1978 in order to support the formation of the Broad Opposition Front (FAO). They are greeted by thousands of Nicaraguans. This Front is formed by the Group of Twelve, nine political parties, and three union federations.

JULY

17 - The United Peoples' Movement (MPU) is formed as a mass front and with the active participation of the three FSLN factions and the Communist Party of Nicaragua.

AUGUST

22 - The *terceristas* take over the National Palace. They leave for Panama with 83 freed political prisoners.

29 - Somoza's air force bombs Matagalpa after a number of strikes begin which affect the whole country. An insurrection of youth is precipitated in the city. A representative of U.S. President Carter arrives in Managua.

SEPTEMBER

9 - The FSLN calls for insurrection. The National Guard unleashes attacks against the civilian population in different cities.

15 - Venezuela signs a defense pact with Costa Rica.

20 - The FSLN is forced to retreat back into the mountains. The insurrection ends with more than 6,000 dead.

22 - The OAS demands that the Interamerican Human Rights Commission write a report *in situ* about the violation of human rights in Nicaragua. A mediating commission of the OAS is proposed, made up of representatives from the United States, Guatemala, and the Dominican Republic.

28 - Somoza officially accepts mediation. All three FSLN factions pronounce themselves against it.

OCTOBER
7 - The OAS mediating commission begins work. It attempts to negotiate a "*Somocismo* without Somoza." The Group of Twelve, the PLI, and the Peoples' Social Christian Party (PPSC) leave the Broad Opposition Front.

NOVEMBER
21 - Costa Rica breaks off relations with Nicaragua.
24 - The Broad Opposition Front asks for the OAS to put Somoza on trial for mass murder.

1979

JANUARY
11 - The OAS mediation group proposes the holding of a plebiscite under international supervision. The Broad Opposition Front and the government reject this idea.

FEBRUARY
1 - The National Patriotic Front (FPN) is formed by the MPU, the Twelve, the PCN, the PLI, the PPSC, and a faction of the Nicaraguan Workers' Confederation (CTN). The Nicaraguan Socialist Party (PSN) remains with the Broad Opposition Front.
8 - The Carter administration reduces its diplomatic relations with Somoza and cancels military aid.
16 - The three FSLN factions unite and form a joint leadership body.

MAY
14 - The International Monetary Fund (IMF) grants Somoza a credit line of $65 million.
20 - Mexico breaks off relations with Nicaragua.
29 - The FSLN announces the final offensive and launches attacks on the Northern and Southern fronts.

JUNE
4 - The FSLN calls for a revolutionary general strike and for a business strike.
16 - The formation of the Provisional Government is announced in Costa Rica. It is made up of Daniel Ortega Saavedra (FSLN), Sergio Ramírez Mercado (the Twelve), Moisés Hassan (MPU), Alfonso Robelo (Broad Opposition Front), and Violeta Chamorro (widow of Pedro J. Chamorro).
22 - The United States calls for a meeting of the OAS and asks for the military intervention of a peace-keeping force in Nicaragua. The proposal is rejected and the OAS asks that Somoza step down.

JULY

6 - Somoza announces that he is willing to step down.

12 - In Punto Arenas, Costa Rica, Carlos Andrés Pérez (President of Venezuela) and Rodrigo Carazo (President of Costa Rica) meet to try to find an alternative political arrangement for Nicaragua.

15 - The FSLN controls León, Masaya, Matagalpa, Diriamba, and other small cities.

16 - Estelí is liberated.

17 - Somoza flees the country. In agreement with the United States, he leaves Francisco Urcuyo in power with the commitment to negotiate with the Provisional Government. Urcuyo announces that he will remain as President until 1981.

19 - The FSLN enters Managua and is received by the people with jubilation.

20 - The Government Junta of National Reconstruction (JGRN) enters Managua from León. The Fundamental Statute of the Republic is enacted. It annuls the *Somocista* Constitution and dissolves the National Guard and the other structures of *Somocista* power. It defines as State powers the five-member JGRN which has Executive Power and shares Legislative Power with the Council of State which is made up of 33 representatives of political parties, unions, cooperative organizations, and the Justice Tribunals.

Decree No. 3 is promulgated. All the properties of the Somoza family and of military officers and government officials who left the country after December 1977 are confiscated. This allows for the formation of the Area of People's Property (APP).

Decree No. 6. Law to Create the Ministries of the State. The following ministers are named: Tomás Borge (Ministry of the Interior); Miguel D'Escoto (Ministry of Foreign Affairs); Bernardino Larios (Ministry of Defense); Joaquín Cuadra Chamorro (Ministry of Finance); Noel Rivas Gasteazoro (Ministry of Industry and Commerce); Manuel José Torres (Ministry of Agricultural Development); Roberto Mayorga (Ministry of Planning); Dionisio Marenco (Ministry of Transport and Public Works); Virgilio Godoy (Ministry of Labor); César Amador Kühl (Ministry of Health); Carlos Tünnermann (Ministry of Education); Ernesto Cardenal (Ministry of Culture); Miguel E. Vigil (Ministry of Housing and Human Settlements); Lea Guido (Ministry of Social Welfare); Alfredo César (Secretary-General of the JGRN); Ernesto Castillo (Attorney General).

22 - Decree No. 10. Law of National Emergency. It penalizes economic crimes. Special Emergency Tribunals are created in order to attend to the cases of violation of this law. It is repealed on April 29, 1980.

26 - The Sandinista Workers' Central (CST) is officially formed.

Decree No. 25. Nationalization of the National Financial System.

Decree No. 26. The Nicaraguan Agrarian Reform Institute (INRA) is created. Comandante Jaime Wheelock is named as minister.

28 - The formation of the General Command of the Sandinista Peoples' Army (EPS) is announced. Comandantes Luis Carrión, Tomás Borge, and Humberto Ortega are its members.

AUGUST
6 - Decree No. 32. Nationalization of Foreign Trade.

8 - Decree No. 38. Extension of Decree No. 3. Confiscation of the properties of supporters and relatives of Somoza.

10 - It is officially announced that in 1980 a National Literacy Crusade will be carried out in order to reach 650,000 illiterate people over the age of ten.

16 - The daily newspaper *La Prensa* reappears.

21 - Decree No. 52. Statute of the Rights and Guarantees of Nicaraguans. The death penalty is abolished.

22 - Decree No. 53. The Sandinista Peoples' Army (EPS) is created.

24 - Decree No. 55. Law of the Defense of the National Currency. The 500 and 1,000 *córdoba* bills are taken out of circulation in order to recover money stolen by *Somocistas*.

25 - Establishment of State control over natural resources (mineral, maritime, and forestry). On November 2, 1979, the foreign mining companies (Gold Mining Inc., Rosita Mine Co., and Neptune Mine Co.) are nationalized.

27 - A Cuban delegation visits Nicaragua and an agreement is signed for cooperation in the field of education; 1,000 Cuban teachers will be sent for two years, Nicaraguan students will receive scholarships to study in Cuba, and advisors will be provided to the Ministry of Education.

SEPTEMBER
27 - Comandante Daniel Ortega in representation of the JGRN speaks at the United Nations and calls for support for the reconstruction of Nicaragua. He proposes that the foreign debt contracted by Somoza be assumed by the most developed countries, in the first place, by those who financed Somoza.

30 - University education becomes free.

OCTOBER
11 - The Ministry of Foreign Trade is formed under the leadership of Alejandro Martínez Cuenca. It is made up of the following Nicaraguan Companies: for Basic Foodstuffs (ENABAS); of Coffee (ENCAFE); of Cotton (ENAL); of Meat (ENCAR); of Agricultural Inputs (ENIA); of Sugar (ENAZUCAR); and of Sea Products (ENMAR). It takes the place of the Institute of Foreign Trade. Trade in petroleum (excepting the ESSO refinery) is nationalized and the company PETRONIC is formed and put in charge of setting prices for distribution.

21 - The census of illiterate people is begun with the participation of more than 2,500 volunteer census takers from the mass organizations.

31 - Decree No. 136. Creation of the National Financial System and its High Council, centralizing the coordination of financial policy.

NOVEMBER

14 - A meeting is held between COSEP (Superior Council for Private Enterprise) and the JGRN. COSEP President Enrique Dreyfuss reports on his trip to the United States in order to support Nicaragua's request for loans from the Interamerican Development Bank (IADB), the World Bank, and the U.S. Agency for International Development.

21 - Decree No. 172. Suspends Decree No. 38 about confiscations for an indefinite time.

29 - Decree No. 179. Creation of the Fund to Fight Unemployment. Financed by freezing payment of the "thirteenth month" (an annual salary bonus) over the minimum wage level.

DECEMBER

12 - The U.S. House of Representatives approves a loan for $75 million to Nicaragua with an amendment calling for suspension of the loan "if Cuban or Soviet troops are deployed in the country."

20 - Decree No. 216. Law of Rent. Rents are reduced by 50 percent and tenants' rights are specified.

27 - Decree No. 223. Reform to the Law to Create the Ministries of State. The Cabinet is restructured and the following government ministers are named: Comandante Humberto Ortega (Ministry of Defense); Comandante Henry Ruiz (Ministry of Planning); Fernando Guzmán (Ministry of Industry); Paul Atha Ramírez (Ministry of Domestic Commerce); Alejandro Martínez Cuenca (Ministry of Foreign Trade); Carlos Shutze (Ministry of Construction); Comandante Jaime Wheelock (Ministry of Agricultural Development).

1980

JANUARY

5 - Decree No. 230. Law to regulate the leasing of lands for the cultivation of cotton.

14 - COSEP supports the economic program.

30 - The U.S. Senate approves the $75 million loan.

31 - Decree No. 263. Law to regulate the leasing of lands for the cultivation of basic grains.

FEBRUARY

5 - A list of prices for 11 basic products is approved.

15 - Meeting of cotton producers with officials of the Ministry of Agricultural Development (MIDA) and the Agrarian Reform Institute (INRA). Commitments are made to raise production, but the need to establish clear rules is put forward: 1) maintain private property; 2) a Law of Protection *(Amparo);* 3) no additional taxes; 4) No more land takeovers;

5) return of machinery not affected by Decree No. 3; and 6) participation in the decisions of State related to agriculture.

22 - Decree No. 323. Law of Defense of the Consumer. Empowers the Ministry of Domestic Commerce to set or freeze prices of foodstuffs and other basic products and their inputs; and to watch over supply, to apply fines, and in the case of repeat offenses, to temporarily or definitively close commercial establishments.

24 - A $50 million agreement for cooperation and technical aid is signed by Cuba and Nicaragua.

25 - The Venezuelan government reaffirms its solidarity with Nicaragua and confirms that it will finance the purchase of $100 million in petroleum.

29 - Decree No. 329. Expropriation of the properties managed by INRA (they will be compensated by handing over certificates or value titles issued by the State for the effects of the Agrarian Reform).

Decree No. 330. Law to prevent and fight the economic decapitalization of the Republic.

MARCH

23 - The National Literacy Crusade begins; 95,832 volunteer literacy workers from all over the country participate.

APRIL

12 - Modification of income tax. For corporations, it goes from being a flexible rate to a fixed 40 percent. For individuals, the marginal rate is raised to 50 percent.

18 - Violeta Chamorro resigns from the JGRN, citing health reasons.

22 - Alfonso Robelo resigns from the JGRN, citing disagreements over the variation of the number of members of the Council of State.

MAY

11 - Alfonso Robelo, in an MDN meeting in Matiguas, talks of "Soviet influence."

13 - The U.S. government conditions the $75 million loan on the replacement of the two JGRN members.

18 - Faced with the resignations of Violeta Chamorro and Alfonso Robelo, the FSLN National Directorate designates and swears in Rafael Córdoba Rivas and Arturo Cruz (both conservatives).

23 - After the murder of literacy worker Georgino Andrade, Comandante Tomás Borge denounces the existence of 32 camps of counter-revolutionaries in Honduras.

AUGUST

18 - The National Literacy Crusade ends. 406,056 people were taught to read and write, reducing the illiteracy rate from 50.35 percent to 12.96 percent.

23 - The FSLN announces that elections will be held in 1985, with the electoral process beginning in 1984.

SEPTEMBER

1 - After a number of months of negotiating the foreign trade debt, the first agreements are signed with banks representing 115 creditors. This renegotiation incorporates unprecedented concessions from the banks.

2 - The government grants financing of 300 million *córdobas* for the reactivation of the private sector.

12 - Carter approves the $75 million in economic aid for Nicaragua.

17 - Somoza is assassinated in Paraguay.

NOVEMBER

4 - Ronald Reagan is elected President of the United States.

11 - COSEP makes public its "analysis of the execution of the Program of the Government of National Reconstruction" in which it states that the government "has stopped being a pluralistic government of national unity and has become a government of one party, the FSLN."

12 - COSEP withdraws from the Council of State.

15 - The Socialist International, meeting in Madrid, creates the International Committee for the Defense of the Nicaraguan Revolution.

17 - Jorge Salazar (Vice-president of COSEP) dies in an armed confrontation with the General Office of State Security (DGSE). He was surprised while transporting weapons which had been collected in order to effect a counterrevolutionary conspiracy. A number of COSEP leaders are arrested and the daily *La Prensa* is censored.

22 - Standard Fruit suspends its purchases of Nicaraguan bananas.

1981

JANUARY

13 - The government concludes negotiations for an arrangement with Standard Fruit and it is agreed that over a period of five years, the company will be acquired by the government.

20 - Ronald Reagan is sworn in as President of the United States.

21 - The United States withholds the last $15 million disbursement of the $75 million loan.

FEBRUARY

23 - The U.S. State Department publishes a White Paper on El Salvador in which it is stated that Nicaragua is involved in arms traffic to Salvadoran guerrillas. In a February 11, 1981 communiqué, the Foreign Ministry denies these accusations.

MARCH

4 - Decree No. 663. The composition of the JGRN is modified: Daniel Ortega (coordinator); Rafael Córdoba Rivas; and Sergio Ramírez. Arturo Cruz is named Nicaraguan ambassador to the United States.

8 - The U.S. embassy in Managua confirms that it will not provide a $9.6 million loan for the purchase of wheat.

9 - The Program of Peoples' Basic Education is begun in order to give follow-up to the people who recently learned to read and write. Around 20,000 volunteer teachers and 150,000 alumni of the Peoples' Education Collectives enroll.

19 - *The Washington Post* reports on the existence of training camps for Nicaraguan counterrevolutionaries in Florida.

23 - Holland grants a $17 million loan to Nicaragua.

30 - The FSLN extends an invitation to the different political, economic, and social groups to attend a process of discussions in order to analyze the situation of the country and to find alternatives which would contribute to the policy of national unity.

APRIL

1 - Libya grants a cash loan of $100 million to Nicaragua.

4 - Decree No. 696. Creation of the Ministry of Agricultural Development and Agrarian Reform (MIDINRA) in order to replace MIDA and INRA.

24 - The FSLN meets with political groups and asks them to sign a joint document in response to the foreign aggression. The parties insist on discussing domestic political problems.

25 - The National Union of Farmers and Ranchers (UNAG) is formed. This marks a change in the form of organization of small- and medium-sized producers who earlier had been part of the Association of Workers of the Countryside (ATC).

MAY

1 - Incentives for cotton production are announced. Import taxes are eliminated and credit amounting to 100 percent of the financeable costs is granted.

13 - At Nicaragua's initiative, a meeting is held of the Heads of State of Nicaragua and Honduras at the El Guasule border post in order to analyze the problems occurring along their common border. They agree that any differences should be resolved through dialogue.

26 - The first shipment of Soviet wheat arrives.

JULY

2 - Nineteen agreements are reached in the National Forum. Among them are: the original character of the process; the democratic, popular, pluralist, and anti-imperialist nature of the process; and that *Somocismo* and imperialist intervention are the causes of economic and social backwardness.

8 - Comandante Edén Pastora leaves Nicaragua, declaring that he will join in the fight of other peoples.

19 - Decree No. 760. Appropriation by the State of abandoned properties. Unless former owners can demonstrate a good cause for having left, abandoned properties are defined as those owned by "Nicaraguans who have left or are leaving the country and have not returned after six months."

Decree No. 782. Law of Agrarian Reform. Limits private property in cases of idleness, deficient exploitation, or abandonment of lands.

Decree No. 759. Confiscation of 15 companies because their "owners committed offenses against the development of the national economy."

Decree No. 769. Nationalization of sugar distribution.

AUGUST

28 - Decree No. 805. Reforms to the Law of Decapitalization, broadening the description of crimes that can be penalized and enacting that procedures "can be initiated with a denouncement that the workers interpose to the Ministry of Justice."

SEPTEMBER

9 - Decree No. 812. Law of the State of Economic and Social Emergency. For a period of one year in order to guarantee a climate of stability and domestic order for economic reconstruction. In the period 1980-81, the Ministry of Planning (MIPLAN) estimated that capital flight was $205 million in addition to the estimate made by the Economic Commission for Latin America (CEPAL) of $535 million for the period 1977-79.

17 - Decree No. 826. Law of Agricultural Cooperatives. Under the direction of MIDINRA.

23 - The opening of 15 money-changing houses is authorized and the parallel exchange rate is set at 20 *córdobas* to the U.S. dollar. The official rate is 10 *córdobas* to the dollar.

NOVEMBER

6 - The United States applies pressure to block IADB loans to Nicaragua. A request for $30 million is tabled.

14 - Arturo Cruz resigns as Nicaragua's ambassador to the United States and announces that he will return to work with the IADB.

25 - The United States declares that Soviet MIG airplanes have arrived in Cuba for delivery to Nicaragua.

DECEMBER

2 - U.S. Secretary of State Alexander Haig, in a meeting with Nicaraguan Foreign Minister Miguel D'Escoto in Santa Lucia, says he is concerned about the size of the Nicaraguan army and about the "totalitarian tendencies" of the Sandinista government.

1982

Over the course of the year, big public investment projects are begun: the TIMAL sugar complex; the Chiltepe milk project; and the CARTONICA industry.

JANUARY

19 - The United States vetoes the IADB loan of $500 million for Nicaragua.

29 - The Export Incentives Program (PIE) is announced. Agro-export producers will receive a portion of the value of their exports in *córdobas* at the official exchange rate of 10 *córdobas* to the U.S. dollar and the rest in a Certificate of Availability of Foreign Exchange (CDD) at the parallel exchange rate of 28 to 1.

FEBRUARY
7 - A massive campaign against polio is begun with the participation of 70,000 peoples' brigade members.

11 - Decree No. 974. Law of Social Security.

12 - A new basis for export taxes is established linked to international prices. On February 15, 1982, a selective tax is applied to non-essential imports (5 *córdobas* on each dollar imported) in order to pay the public debt.

14 - *The Washington Post* reveals that Reagan has approved a covert operations plan against Nicaragua which includes $19 million to be administered by the Central Intelligence Agency (CIA).

Evacuation is completed of 8,500 Miskito Indians from the banks of the Río Coco along the Nicaragua-Honduras border. They are relocated to Tasba Pri in response to the stepped-up aggression of the counterrevolution in that zone.

18 - The Episcopal Conference condemns the resettling of the Miskitos, alleging "serious violations of human rights."

23 - Reagan launches the "mini Marshall Plan" or Caribbean Basin Initiative of economic and social development for Central America and the Caribbean, excluding Nicaragua.

MARCH
25 - Daniel Ortega speaks to a special session of the U.N. Security Council and demands that the United States stop its aggressive policy against Nicaragua. Twelve of the fifteen countries represented there vote in Nicaragua's favor. The United States vetoes the resolution.

APRIL
1 - Chief of the Honduran Armed Forces, General Gustavo Alvarez, says his country "is not opposed to a possible intervention by the United States in Central America."

15 - Edén Pastora announces in Costa Rica that he has plans to carry out an armed struggle against the Sandinista revolution.

17 - Income and net property taxes are increased by 10 percent.

29 - Decree No. 1040. Extension of the Minimum Wage Law as a result of the emergency situation.

MAY
14 - Alfredo César resigns as President of the Central Bank.

25 - The JGRN forms an emergency committee in order to deal with the serious situation caused all over the country by floods and hurricane-force winds. Damages caused by the natural phenomena were estimated by CEPAL at $519.3 million.

JUNE

7 - Law to regulate commerce and defend the consumer. Empowers the Ministry of Domestic Commerce (MICOIN) to exercise control over all commerce in Nicaragua, including imported goods.

16 - Robelo announces in Panama that he has formed an alliance with Pastora, whom he calls his "armed wing."

JULY

26 - Decree No. 1081. New administrative regionalization of the country in order to improve and decentralize the work of the government. Six regions and three Special Zones are created. Delegates of the JGRN are named to each.

28 - Nicaragua renews its call for negotiations with the United States in a letter delivered to the President of the U.N. Security Council.

31 - The JGRN announces a series of measures aimed at rationalizing the consumption of petroleum derivatives.

Nicaragua and Cuba sign a cooperation agreement for $80 million.

SEPTEMBER

7 - Mexican President López Portillo and Venezuelan President Herrera Campins each send letters to Reagan, Ortega, and Honduran President Suazo Córdoba asking for: an end to the critical situation in Central America; an end to U.S.-Honduran support of Nicaraguan counterrevolutionaries; a reduction of troops in the region; and efforts to be made aimed at reaching a general peace agreement.

16 - The IADB approves a $34.4 million loan to Nicaragua. The United States vetoes it, alleging that the "Nicaraguan macro-economy is not leading to the development of the country."

OCTOBER

12 - It is announced that ENABAS will assume control of the national commerce in rice in order to confront the existing problems of food supply.

16 - The Emergency Commission on unemployment is formed. It counts on a fund to create emergency employment in projects which don't require foreign exchange. Minister of Labor Virgilio Godoy reports that there are between 10,000 and 15,000 unemployed because of the closing of companies due to a lack of raw materials.

19 - Nicaragua is elected to the U.N. Security Council despite strong opposition by the United States.

26 - Standard Fruit announces inopportunely its decision to suspend all activities in Nicaragua, violating the agreement signed with the Nicaraguan government in 1980 in which it had guaranteed to continue to market bananas for a period of five years.

NOVEMBER

1 - Regulation of the Foreign Exchange for Visible Exports. An increase in the percentage paid at the parallel exchange rate through the CDD (selective devaluation). The areas benefitted are cotton, sugar, meat, and tobacco. For industry, the rate remains 60 percent at the official exchange rate and 40 percent at the parallel rate.

30 - Nicaragua and Costa Rica agree to patrol their common border.

Hector Francés, a former Argentinian agent involved in activities against Nicaragua from Costa Rica under the direction of the CIA, reveals a plan aimed at controlling the northeast of the country in order to declare it a "liberated zone" and then proclaim a government-in-exile which would be immediately recognized by the United States, El Salvador, and Argentina.

The Argentinian government grants a $15 million loan.

DECEMBER

8 - The U.S. House of Representatives unanimously approves a ban on the Pentagon and the CIA from training or arming anti-Sandinistas.

1983

Throughout 1983, big investment projects continue to be initiated: Sébaco Valley agro-industrial complex; the Contingency Plan for Basic Grains; Burley Tobacco; and African palm projects on the Atlantic Coast and in the Río San Juan Department.

JANUARY

9 - The Contadora Group is formed by Venezuela, Colombia, Mexico, and Panama.

14 - The Document of Managua is approved by the plenary session of the ministerial meeting of the Non-Aligned Nations Bureau. It condemns the campaign by the United States aimed at overthrowing the government of Nicaragua.

FEBRUARY

4 - Pierre Schori, the Swedish Vice-minister of Foreign Affairs, announces a 50 percent increase in aid to Nicaragua.

24 - In San José, the Foreign Ministers of Costa Rica, Honduras, and El Salvador sign a seven-point declaration calling for a dialogue for peace.

27 - During the Second Meeting of Directors of the National Financial System (SFN), Sergio Ramírez states that a currency devaluation is not under consideration "because that kind of solution would only benefit the minorities."

MARCH

4 - Pope John Paul II visits Nicaragua.

14 - Colombia announces the renewal of trade with Nicaragua after three years of inactivity. A $36 million agreement is signed.

20 - In paid ads in Honduran daily newspapers, the formation of a "Government Junta" is announced. In it, among others, are: Alfonso Callejas Deshon (former Vice-president in the Somoza government); Adolfo Calero (former director of Coca-Cola); Colonel Enrique Bermúdez (former National Guard officer); Alfonso Robelo; Edén Pastora; and Lucia Cardenal de Salazar (widow of Jorge Salazar). They call on the international community to recognize this junta.

APRIL

4 - The Plan of Banking Specialization is begun. The banks will specialize in the giving of attention to different sectors of the economy.

Nicaragua proposes to hold separate talks with the United States and Honduras with the mediation of the Contadora Group. Honduras proposes the OAS as mediator. Contadora accepts and on April 11, the OAS agrees that Contadora should do it. U.S. Ambassador to the United Nations, Jeane Kirkpatrick rejects the possibility of a bilateral dialogue with Nicaragua.

6 - The World Health Organization and UNICEF declare Nicaragua to be "a model country in health."

21 - A new line of credit from Brazil of $10 million is announced.

25 - An agreement is signed with Spain for a $45 million credit line.

MAY

9 - The Reagan administration reduces the sugar import quota from 58,000 to 6,000 metric tons (a 90 percent reduction) and redistributes it among El Salvador, Honduras, and Costa Rica.

10 - Reforms to income taxes. The tax will be differential: 45 percent for commercial activities; 37.5 percent for agro-industry; 35 percent for agriculture; and 40 percent for other activities. A rate of 20 percent is set on distributed dividends.

19 - The U.N. Security Council passes a resolution calling for an end to intervention in Central America and supporting Contadora.

27 - Reforms to bank interest rates. Application of new incentives for the productive sectors.

29 - The JGRN issues three decrees in order to slow down currency destabilization and neutralize the sources of financing for the counterrevolution: Law about Possession, Introduction, and Departure of Foreign Currency; Law about the Departure and Introduction of National Currency; and rules to regulate the buying and selling operations of foreign exchange freely negotiated with the SFN. Six private money-changing houses are closed down.

JUNE

5 - Nicaragua expels three CIA agents operating out of the U.S. embassy in Managua who were involved in a plan to assassinate government leaders. The United States responds by closing down six Nicaraguan consulates. Nicaragua then imposes a visa requirement for U.S. citizens to enter the country.

10 - The management of Borden Chemical and Ismael Reyes Trading, S.A. is taken over by the government. The owner of both, Ismael Reyes, had left the country and was accused of decapitalization.

29 - The United States vetoes a loan for $1.7 million to Nicaragua in the IADB.

JULY

17 - The Presidents of the Contadora countries issue the Cancún Declaration in which they call on Ronald Reagan and Fidel Castro to support the efforts of Contadora. They put forward ten points referring to weapons control and other actions in order to create a climate of reduced tensions and confidence in the Central American area.

AUGUST

10 - The JGRN presents a draft bill for a Law of Patriotic Military Service (SMP) to the Council of State. It is passed on September 13, 1983.

17 - The Council of State passes the Law of Political Parties, the first of its kind in the country.

19 - Comandante Daniel Ortega announces that the debts of campesinos will be forgiven. This had been requested by UNAG, arguing that the drought mainly affected the production of basic grains.

A meeting of the Socialist International in Río de Janeiro gives support to Nicaragua and condemns the maneuvering of the United States in the region.

27 - The Momotombo geothermal electricity plant is inaugurated. It cost $42 million and can generate 35 megawatts.

29 - The Episcopal Conference issues a communiqué in which it comes out against the SMP.

SEPTEMBER

8 - UNESCO awards Nicaragua an honorable mention for its successes in the literacy and adult education programs.

9 - Two T-28 combat planes bomb the port of Corinto.

22 - The U.S. Senate Intelligence Committee gives approval to Reagan's $19 million plan to continue financing the counterrevolution.

OCTOBER

1 - At the initiative of General Paul Gorman, Chief of the Southern Command of the U.S. Army, the military chiefs of Guatemala, Honduras, and El Salvador meet in Guatemala to discuss the possibility of reactivating the CONDECA defense pact.

4 - The Executive Table of the U.N. General Assembly receives a request from Nicaragua to include the theme of Central America in its agenda in spite of opposition from the United States. It is seconded by Costa Rica, El Salvador, Honduras, and Guatemala.

5 - A new tax on the business dealings of *buhoneros*: 10 percent tax for imports and 20 percent on exports.

10 - Nicaraguan Democratic Force (FDN) commandos burn fuel storage facilities in the port of Corinto; 1,500 people have to be evacuated by the Civil Defense.

14 - Exxon announces that it will no longer lease boats to Nicaragua for shipping Mexican petroleum, citing the risk of damages to them.

The JGRN announces new emergency measures in order to deal with the escalation in aggression: acquire weapons for defense; save energy; ration fuel; organize production battalions (voluntary brigades to bring in the harvest); place priority on defense in the supply of foodstuffs, clothing, and footwear; guard economic targets; promote the territorial organization of peoples' militias; and save foreign exchange.

NOVEMBER

11 - The U.N. General Assembly adopts by consensus a resolution asking for an end to "acts of aggression" against Nicaragua and it encourages "democratic and representative systems" in Central America.

17 - The U.S. Congress approves an additional $24 million for support to the counterrevolution which must be spent by the CIA before July 1984.

23 - The tax for non-essential imports is doubled, going from 5 to 10 *córdobas* for each dollar.

DECEMBER

24 - COSEP issues the document "A step towards democracy: free elections." COSEP and the parties of the Nicaraguan Democratic Coordinator (CDN) threaten not to participate in the elections unless their conditions are met.

1984

JANUARY

7 - The Contadora Group holds its fifth joint meeting with the five Central American Foreign Ministers who agree to implement a plan for complying with the 21 points agreed to in September 1983.

FEBRUARY

21 - The JGRN announces that the date for elections is moved ahead to November 4, 1984.

24 - CIA commandos mine the Nicaraguan port of El Bluff. In March, they mine the port of Corinto.

MARCH

8 - The parties of the CDN walk out of the discussions on the Electoral Law because their proposals aren't accepted.

12 - It is announced that the United States has decided to send a new war fleet to the Caribbean coast of Nicaragua.

UNAG president Wilberto Lara asks for greater participation in the discussion of the 1984 Economic Plan because his organization makes up an important component of agricultural production.

15 - The Council of State passes the Electoral Law.

19 - Fifteen socialist leaders from Europe say that it is a duty for all democrats to promote and support the electoral process in Nicaragua.

22 - The COSEP President calls on the political parties to boycott the elections.

APRIL

4 - In the U.N. Security Council, the United States vetoes a draft resolution which is supported by 13 of the 15 members and which condemns the mining of the ports by the CIA and supports Contadora.

9 - Nicaragua presents a demand to the World Court of Justice at the Hague that the United States be condemned for the mining of icaragua's ports and the support given to the counterrevolution.

MAY

10 - The World Court orders the United States to end the mining of Nicaraguan ports and the support it gives to the counterrevolutionary forces, actions which act against the "sovereignty and political independence" of Nicaragua.

31 - MICOIN announces a 50 percent reduction in subsidies to the products in the basic shopping basket. Subsidies are maintained on sugar and milk. The distribution channels for rice, soap, sorghum, cooking oil, and salt are nationalized. The supply of eight products is guaranteed by means of ration cards. All increases in prices paid to producers will be passed on to consumers.

JUNE

9 - Contadora delivers the "Document of Contadora for Peace and Cooperation in Central America" to the Central American governments.

25 - The United States and Nicaragua begin talks in Manzanillo, Mexico. The United States withdraws on January 18, 1985.

AUGUST

1 - The electoral campaign officially begins.

2 - MICOIN announces the setting of prices for 21 basic products and takes charge of the distribution and sale of 12.

8 - The JGRN issues decrees in which recourse to legal protection (*amparo*) and the right to strike are restored. The law regulating information with an economic content is repealed.

17 - The United States presents its statement to the World Court, arguing that this tribunal is not the appropriate forum for hearing cases dealing with armed aggression. On November 26, 1984, the Court declares itself competent in relation to hearing the Nicaraguan suit against the United States.

SEPTEMBER

21 - Nicaragua announces its decision to "accept in its totality and sign immediately any modification" to the Revised Contadora Document of September 7, 1984.

24 - Sale is begun in supermarkets of products which are in short supply in the assured channels. These products are sold with no limit on quantity at prices higher than the official ones but lower than those of the black market.

OCTOBER

1 - A program of dollar incentives for livestock producers comes into effect. Later, this measure is extended to cotton and coffee growers.

4 - The first phase of the implementation of the National System of Organization of Labor and Salaries (SNOTS) is finished and revision begins.

The U.S. Senate approves a request by Reagan for $28 million in order to support the counterrevolution.

30 - The PLI formally asks to withdraw from the elections because of an internal division of the party. Constantino Pereira, PLI Vice-presidential candidate, announces that he won't withdraw his candidacy. On November 2, 1984, Virgilio Godoy announces that he, too, will go into the elections, although under duress. U.S. gunboats trail European merchant ships which dock in Nicaraguan harbors.

NOVEMBER

4 - The first free elections are held in Nicaragua. The results are: FSLN - 67.2 percent; Democratic Conservative Party (PCD) - 14 percent; Independent Liberal Party (PLI) - 9.6 percent; People's Social Christian Party (PPSC) - 5.6 percent; Communist Party of Nicaragua (PCN) - 1.5 percent; Socialist Party of Nicaragua (PSN) - 1.3 percent; and the Popular Action Movement - Marxist-Leninist (MAP-ML) - 1 percent.

6 - Reagan is reelected as President of the United States. That same day, the United States threatens Nicaragua with direct military action, alleging that the USSR is sending 18 MIG planes to Nicaragua.

9 - Spy flights of the "black bird" (supersonic SR-71) begin over Nicaraguan territory.

12 - A national state of military alert is declared.

30 - The participating organizations decide to suspend the National Dialogue indefinitely. The Social Christian Party (PSC) calls for new elections in 1986.

DECEMBER

13 - Honduras announces that is has reached an agreement with the United States to set up a permanent U.S. military base in its territory.

24 - New decrees affecting taxes are issued. A General Value Tax is initiated of 10 percent over the value of imports and the leasing of goods and services. For restaurants, hotels, and others it is 15 percent. Selective

Consumer Tax is extended to 400 products and the rate is increased by between 10 percent and 100 percent depending on whether the product is national or imported. Capital gains tax is set as a progressive tax on increases in the value of properties. A rate of 7.5 percent is set for net capital gains. The law of assumed income establishes the assumed amount of annual income for professionals with private practices and some services.

1985

JANUARY
1 - The Mexican government suspends credit for supplying petroleum because Nicaragua cannot pay the debt accumulated. In 1982, Venezuela had suspended petroleum supplies for the same reason.
3 - Arturo Cruz asks Washington to renew official aid to the counterrevolution.
10 - Comandante Daniel Ortega and Sergio Ramírez assume the Presidency and Vice-presidency of the Republic.

  The National Assembly is inaugurated. A pluralistic executive body is elected with representatives from the FSLN, PCD, PPSC, PSN, and PLI.

FEBRUARY
8 - Macroeconomic adjustment measures are announced: devaluation (from 10 *córdobas* to the U.S. dollar to 28 to 1 for visible trade; 40 to 1 and 50 to 1 for invisible exports; 20 to 1 for essential consumption); elimination of 50 percent of the subsidy to basic consumption products; reduction and rationalization of public investments; wage increases; free and official markets for dollars; and more. The goals were: to encourage production; to adjust salaries periodically in line with the reactivation of the economy; and to redirect resources in order to guarantee defense and improve supplies to the rural areas.
11 - The "Iron Fist" operation is carried out against speculators and profiteers.

MARCH
24 - MICOIN roadblocks to check for the unauthorized transfer of products from one region to another are lifted in order to permit free circulation of the produce of campesinos in the cities.
25 - In the IADB Assembly, Nicaragua protests and denounces the boycott waged by the United States against the $58.4 million loan for agriculture which is submitted to "restudy" by that agency. (U.S. Secretary of State George Shultz had sent a letter to the IADB on January 30, 1985 objecting to the loan and stating that its approval would make it difficult for the United States to make new contributions to the IADB.) Ten nations back up Nicaragua.

APRIL

4 - Reagan, meeting with Arturo Cruz, Adolfo Calero, and Alfonso Robelo, presents "a plan for Nicaragua" which includes a proposal for a "national dialogue" and conditions the use of $14 million of support to the "democratic resistance" on the initiation of this dialogue within 60 days.

15 - UNAG criticizes the government for its errors in handling the marketing of perishable products.

18 - The Socialist International issues a declaration condemning Reagan's "peace plan."

24 - The U.S. Congress votes against the "peace plan."

MonseÉor Miguel Obando y Bravo is named as Cardinal by the Pope.

26 - Daniel Ortega travels to the USSR in order to ensure the supply of petroleum to substitute for the shipments suspended by Mexico.

MAY

1 - The Reagan administration declares an economic embargo against Nicaragua.

10 - The government announces new measures which continue the macroeconomic adjustment begun in February: new guaranteed prices for agricultural products with dollar incentives for agro-exports and the opening of money-changing houses and new, more liberal, regulations for foreign exchange. At the same time, steps are announced for confronting the U.S. blockade: austerity and rationalization of the use of resources; self-supply of substitutable spare parts; support to innovators who design ways to substitute spare parts; etc.

A resolution of the U.N. Security Council demands that the United States immediately lift the trade embargo imposed on Nicaragua. The United States vetoes the resolution.

17 - Nicaragua officially proposes to the United States the renewal of the talks in Manzanillo in June.

JUNE

1 - Payment of wages in kind (giving workers some of the products that they produce) is abolished. This had been used by companies in order to get around the wage freeze.

12 - Calero, Cruz, and Robelo, supported by the CDN, form the United Nicaraguan Opposition (UNO) in Panama as "the leading body of the efforts of democratic Nicaraguans on all the fronts of struggle."

19 - The Tegucigalpa Bloc (Honduras, El Salvador, and Costa Rica) break up the meeting of Contadora, refusing to give priority to discussion of the blockade and military aggression against Nicaragua.

27 - At the 40th meeting of COMECON in Warsaw, it is announced that more aid will be given to Nicaragua through soft loans and collaboration in three important areas: agriculture, livestock production, and textiles.

JULY
25 - The U.S. Congress ratifies the approval of $27 million for the counter-revolution.

AUGUST
25 - The first meeting held between Contadora and the Support Group (Brazil, Argentina, Uruguay, and Peru) in Cartegena ends.

SEPTEMBER
9 - The Reagan administration begins a diplomatic offensive throughout Latin America with visits by itinerant ambassador Harry Schlaudeman. It aims to influence the next meeting of Contadora and the Support Group. Strong pressures are applied to Honduras, El Salvador, and Costa Rica so that they won't sign the declaration.

OCTOBER
8 - Contadora meets. The Central American foreign ministers, following U.S. orientations, block the signing of the declaration.

11 - The government of Ecuador breaks off relations with Nicaragua.

15 - A State of Emergency is decreed. Thirteen articles of the Statute of Rights and Guarantees are suspended for one year in order to prevent the formation of an internal front organized by the CIA.

17 - Holland and Spain express regrets about the State of Emergency.

24 - The European Parliament calls the U.S. policy towards Nicaragua "a conscious attempt to push a country into dictatorship" and says it regrets that "continued outside pressures" have obliged the Nicaraguan government "to limit political and union freedoms."

NOVEMBER
1 - Serious losses and damages are caused by floods all over the country.

10 - Nicaragua announces that it won't sign the Contadora declaration if the U.S. government doesn't commit itself formally to ending the aggression in all its forms.

11 - The Second Conference in Luxembourg between the European Economic Community (EEC), Spain, Portugal, and the nations of Central America is held. The EEC-Central America declaration contains a $35 million cooperation plan for the five Central American countries.

17 - Spain confirms the granting of $35 million in credit and food aid to Nicaragua.

DECEMBER
2 - Law of Monetary Discipline, Opening of Accounts, and Limits for Cash Transactions. The goal is to promote the practice of payment in checks for economic transactions and to facilitate monetary control by the government.

6 - Nicaragua establishes diplomatic relations with the People's Republic of China.

8 - The 11th Conference of the Latin American Economic System (SELA), held in Cartegena, agrees to condemn the embargo against Nicaragua.

1986

JANUARY

1 - A salary increase is made in order to benefit workers in directorship positions, professionals, and technicians, as well as urban and agricultural workers.

9 - The Nicaraguan Institute of Social Services and Welfare (INSSBI) announces that coverage has been extended to over half the population, the highest level ever in Nicaraguan history.

11 - President-elect of Honduras, José Azcona, admits that there are Nicaraguan counterrevolutionaries in Honduran territory.

The government makes amendments to the Law of Agrarian Reform, eliminating the limits set earlier for taking over idle farms and those that are exploited deficiently or are being leased, without this affecting the rights of those who work their farms efficiently. It implies that inefficient medium-scale agricultural producers can be affected by the agrarian reform in order to make room for small producers with insufficient or no land.

12 - The Contadora Group and the Support Group, meeting in Carabellada, Venezuela, urge the United States to renew talks with Nicaragua and end support to the counterrevolutionary forces.

14 - The five Central American foreign ministers, meeting in Guatemala, sign the Guatemala Declaration in which they support the declaration made in Carabellada. Spain, together with 13 Latin American countries, supports it as well and seeks to find more support in the EEC. The OAS and EEC give their support to the Carabellada and Guatemala declarations at a later date.

17 - U.S. State Department spokesman Bernard Kalb says that the United States does not accept the terms of the peace message from Carabellada.

31 - The Central Bank of Nicaragua announces new exchange rates. The rates for imports and exports are unified and the legal rate is devalued to 70 *córdobas* to the U.S. dollar. Savings account interest rates are increased substantially.

FEBRUARY

5 - COSEP publishes a letter sent to the Minister of Agriculture and Agrarian Reform which rejects the amendments made to the Law of Agrarian Reform.

17 - A delegation of 22 Guatemalan businesspeople arrives in Managua in what is called an "offensive to reactivate bilateral trade for the benefit of the two nations."

25 - Reagan formally requests that the U.S. Congress approve a $100 million contra aid package, $70 million of which is for military aid to be administered by the State Department, the CIA, or the Pentagon.

28 - The Communiqué of Punta del Este, signed by the foreign ministers of the Contadora and Support Group countries, reaffirms the terms of the Declaration of Carabellada.

MARCH

9 - The government announces a set of policies for the prices of petroleum products, electricity, water, transport services, prices to producers and consumers, and a new salary increase.

11 - Leaders of the ATC and the CST outline a series of actions to take in order to ensure the success of the new economic measures.

17 - The ministerial resolution of the Unified Health System goes into effect. Patients will begin to pay the cost price of medicines in all the pharmacies, health centers, and hospitals.

20 - By a narrow margin of 12 votes (222 against, 210 for) and after hours of debate, the U.S. House of Representatives rejects Reagan's request for $100 million for the contras.

APRIL

9 - The Honduran Minister of the Economy arrives in Nicaragua to discuss the possibility of increasing trade between the two countries. Afterwards, on May 15, 1986, a treaty is signed in which both governments agree to set up a bilateral Clearing House with up to $15 million for the purchase by barter of Honduran and Nicaraguan products.

11 - Nicaragua responds to the Contadora Group and agrees to sign the June 6 peace document "so long as by that date, the U.S. aggression against Nicaragua has ended."

25 - The government announces new prices for agro-export products and a new method of giving dollar incentives for increases in productivity.

JUNE

20 - The West German government announces that it won't renew its aid to Nicaragua, which had been suspended in 1984.

22 - The Resolution of the XVII Congress of the Socialist International held in Lima, Peru agrees "to reject the Reagan administration's policy of destabilization, economic blockade, and pro-military aid" to the Nicaraguan contras.

24 - Reagan makes a direct appeal to U.S. citizens on radio and TV that they support his request for $100 million for the "freedom fighters."

25 - The U.S. House of Representatives approves (249 for, 174 against) $100 million for the Nicaraguan counterrevolutionaries and authorizes the CIA to direct operations against Nicaragua.

27 - The World Court hands down its verdict with respect to the accusation made by Nicaragua on April 9, 1984 and condemns the U.S. government as an aggressor government, obliging it to pay compensation to Nicaragua for damages caused as result of the aggression, and to end that aggression immediately. The United States says that it will ignore the ruling. Nicaragua calls for an urgent meeting of the U.N. Security

Council on July 1 in order to examine the Court's ruling and the approval by the U.S. Congress of the $100 million in contra aid.

AUGUST

1 - The United States vetoes the draft resolution presented to the U.N. Security Council that asks it to support the World Court ruling.

2 - Political parties represented in the National Assembly give their approval to the suit brought by Nicaragua to the World Court against Honduras and Costa Rica for the use of their territory to launch attacks against Nicaragua.

14 - The U.S. Senate approves (53 for, 47 against) the giving of $100 million to the CIA mercenaries ($70 million for weapons and $30 million for logistical support).

20 - Nicaragua proposes a seven-point plan in the meeting of Ministers Responsible for Economic Integration in order to strengthen economic cooperation and find mechanisms which would alleviate the impact of the international economic crisis: 1) Search for financing for industrial production and technological renovation of the industrial plant of Central America. 2) Financing from the Central American Bank of Economic Integration (BCIE). 3) Joint initiatives for preferential treatment for the export products of the five countries. 4) Joint exploitation of the natural resources in border areas. 5) Make the systems of trade relations more flexible. This proposal was accepted by the ministers as a basis for the establishment of a new framework of economic integration in Central America. At this meeting, Nicaragua reactivates trade with Costa Rica and Guatemala on the basis of a bilateral Clearing House.

SEPTEMBER

3 - The conclusions of the VIII Summit of the Non-Aligned Nations back Nicaragua's suit that the United States respect international legislation and end its campaign of aggression. Dialogue is called for.

19 - The U.S. House of Representatives bans the use of secret funds by the CIA. This action is linked to the request for $100 million.

27 - The National Agrarian Reform Council is created.

OCTOBER

3 - The *Miami Herald* reports that the Pentagon has made official a document called "The Project of the Collective Low Intensity Conflict."

7 - A camouflaged military airplane from the United States is shot down over Nicaragua in the Río San Juan department. U.S. citizen Eugene Hassenfus is captured and will be tried in Nicaraguan courts. Two pilots die. Afterwards, it is discovered that this event was linked to the Iran-contra scandal.

14 - Río San Juan is declared the first territory free of campesinos without land.

22 - The Nicaraguan government files a suit in the U.S. court in the district of San Francisco, California against the Standard Fruit Company for more than $35 million.

NOVEMBER
19 - The National Assembly approves the National Constitution after 49 days of debate.
26 - Scandal rocks the White House. Reagan announces the dismissal of Vice-admiral John Poindexter, a member of the National Security Council, and his aide, Lieutenant-Colonel Oliver North. He accuses them of redirecting between $10 million and $30 million to Swiss bank accounts held by contras. These resources came from the sale of arms to Iran, by way of Israel, in exchange for hostages in Lebanon.

1987

JANUARY
5 - Reagan decides to increase the amount he is requesting from the U.S. Congress for financial resources to the counterrevolution to $105 million for the fiscal year.
26 - The Nicaraguan government begins a process of fusion and specialization of companies in the manufacturing industries—primarily in textiles, clothing, and footwear—in order to increase productivity and reduce costs.

FEBRUARY
21 - 270 European parliamentarians call on the U.S. Congress not to grant more funds to the contras.
26 - The *Washington Post* reports that National Security Council member Frank Carlucci is considering imposing a naval blockade on Nicaragua in order to stop "the flow of Soviet aid" to Nicaragua.

MICOIN explains the policy of setting up roadblocks to prevent unauthorized traffic of basic products within the country.

MARCH
5 - The Finance Ministry announces fiscal measures aimed at bringing in more revenues: freezing the profits of establishments which don't pay their taxes; increasing taxes for some sectors, particularly professionals, private practices, and agricultural cooperatives; and demanding that APP companies bring themselves up to date with their tax payments. An increase of the tax base to 30,000 more taxpayers is the goal.
7 - Daniel Ortega sends a letter to the member countries of the International Coffee Organization proposing the creation of a Latin American Front, a new meeting of the organization be held, and an airing of different points of view leading to the normalization of international coffee prices.
9 - Restrictions are placed on the importation of luxury vehicles.

15 - Energetic actions to deal with the economic and social crises of the peoples of Central America are asked of the Presidents of the region by the ministers in charge of economic integration in a meeting in Managua. "We need to reverse the strong contraction of inter-regional trade, improve the mechanisms of payment by means of the rapid implementation of the Central American Right to Importation (DICA) in all the countries of the region and, to the degree possible, utilize national currencies. We consider it necessary to propitiate reactivation and integration, not only in industry, but also in agriculture, transport, tourism, and communications. This would allow for the reinforcement of the complementarity of our economies.

"In regards to the problem of smuggling which is seriously affecting the efforts for economic reactivation because of the disloyal competition that this implies, we consider it necessary to immediately adopt economic measures aimed at regulating overland transport of merchandise in transit coming from outside of the Central American area.

"We believe it is urgently necessary to make efforts in the search for national consensus directed at the rapid reestablishment of negotiations which would allow for the putting into practice of the International Coffee Agreement, as well as negotiations related to international trade.

"Equally important, we believe, is to respect the positions held up to now by each one of our countries with respect to the problem of the foreign debt. The search for minimum consensus is necessary in order to define a general framework for the region which would orient negotiations independently of the countries of the area.

"We are convinced that, in order to attain success in these efforts, it is necessary to strengthen our capacity of coordination on the national level with all the different entities involved in the integration process.

"Mr. Presidents: Being certain that the ideas reflected here would contribute to the process of the reactivation of the economies of Central America and to the well-being of our peoples, and thereby to progress along the road to peace, we respectfully ask you to consider our proposals in your deliberations. Signed: Lizardo A. Soza (Guatemala), José Ricardo Perdomo (El Salvador), Reginaldo Panting (Honduras), Alejandro Martínez Cuenca (Nicaragua), and Luis Diego Escalante (Costa Rica)."

21 - A meeting about coffee begins in Managua between representatives of the different producer countries of Latin America. They agree to draw up a plan of action for the future with the goal of reestablishing the quota system of the International Coffee Organization. The meeting had major importance on the level of Central America. In the words of the Guatemalan Vice-minister of Foreign Affairs, "It means that the countries of Central America have returned to the initiative of holding talks and presenting a common front which, in any case, should be a faithful reflection of the common front we should have in political affairs."

APRIL

9 - The Finance Ministry announces the application of taxes for the informal sector. Taxes charged to producers of rum, beer, cigarettes, and soft drinks are increased.

10 - A deficit in sugar production indicates to Nicaraguan government authorities that the privately owned San Antonio sugar refinery is being badly administered.

26 - Hans Stercken, President of the Council of the Executive Committee of the Interparliamentary Union (IPU), praises the organizational capacity and infrastructure set up by Nicaragua for the celebration of the 77th IPU Conference. "I have never in my life seen a convention center built in such a short time," he says in a press conference.

MAY

1 - The Labor Ministry and the CST propose that the salary policy be decentralized.

3 - The IPU conference ends. It supports Contadora in its efforts to promote the Central American peace process through negotiation. It gives broad support to Nicaragua against the U.S. war of aggression and energetically urges the end of foreign support to the irregular forces.

5 - The government takes measures in order to guarantee minimal supplies of basic goods to salaried workers. Shortages of cooking oil, sugar, rice, and powdered milk are more severe.

8 - A pilot plan of salary incentives for efficiency is put into effect. It only applies to the National Financial System. The maximum incentive is set at 60 percent of the base salary.

30 - The government and workers propose making a national effort to increase productivity.

31 - The Labor Ministry authorizes payment of incentives for efficiency in the companies of the agricultural, industrial, and transport sectors.

JUNE

7 - Daniel Ortega announces economic adjustments and the reinforcing of the defense effort. Salaries are increased by 30 percent. New prices are set for petroleum products and measures are taken for conserving them. A monetary stabilization rate is set and actions are taken to control the prices and supply of 54 basic products.

JULY

2 - The responsibility for the assignation of foreign exchange to private merchants by the money-changing houses is no longer controlled by the Chamber of Commerce and passes to MICOIN. The quota is reduced by 50 percent in order to rationalize the use of foreign exchange.

4 - Nicaragua arranges for petroleum from Iran. Sergio Ramírez makes calls on the international community to give solidarity support in order to obtain petroleum on credit in order to deal with the energy crisis. The first responses were from Cuba (40,000 metric tons) and the USSR (100,000 metric tons).

8 - The Vice-minister of MICOIN announces new increases in the prices of milk, meat, eggs, and rice in order to encourage production.

11 - Comandante Wheelock meets with livestock producers from all over the country—representatives of UNAG and FAGANIC (Federation of Associations of Livestock Producers of Nicaragua)—in order to discuss that sector's problems. The government announces a special credit policy and expresses its willingness to develop a plan of action through the recently created National Livestock Commission, made up of representatives from MIDINRA, MICOIN, the Ministry of Industry, UNAG, FAGANIC, the SFN, and the ATC.

17 - A collective agreement is signed between the Health Ministry (MINSA) and the 26,000 member Health Workers Federation (FETSALUD).

21 - Distribution of tokens for bus transport in Managua is begun in workplaces. This measure seeks to protect the salary of workers in the formal sector of the economy and ensure that the State-run National Bus Company (ENABUS) will be able to collect revenues.

27 - President Oscar Arias of Costa Rica visits Daniel Ortega in a tour of Central American countries. Both presidents express total support for the upcoming presidential summit meeting in Guatemala and highlight the importance of the participation of the Contadora Group.

AUGUST

3 - An 11 percent reduction of fuel consumption is decreed for all institutions. Saturday is no longer a working day in the central administration of the State. On August 30, 1987 the prices for gasoline and diesel are increased by 100 percent.

A new card for the distribution of basic goods is introduced in order to acquire products in the Centers for the Supply of Workers (CAT). The cards are distributed in workplaces and it is sought to assure that priority is placed on supplying workers and reducing speculation and profiteering.

5 - Reagan administration spokespeople propose that the Nicaraguan government talk with the counterrevolution in exchange for the U.S. administration postponing its request to the U.S. Congress for $150 million until September 1987. This proposal is presented as an alternative to the Arias Plan which calls for the simultaneous suspension of foreign military aid to irregular forces, a cease-fire, and the making of efforts to democratize Central America.

6 - Daniel Ortega calls on the U.S. government to begin talks without conditions in Managua, Washington, or any other location in order to discuss the proposals of the United States and Nicaragua.

7 - U.S. Secretary of State George Shultz rejects the call by the Nicaraguan government for the immediate renewal of talks between the two countries and says, "What has to be discussed, has to be done in a regional context."

The Central American presidential summit meeting begins in Guatemala. It ends with the signing of a general agreement called "Procedures for Establishing a Firm and Lasting Peace in Central America." Points contained in the agreement are: 1) dialogue with opposition groups in each country; 2) amnesty and that the irregular forces of each country free all people in their control; 3) formation of National Reconciliation Commissions; 4) an exhortation to end hostilities; 5) democratization; 6) free elections; 7) end of support to irregular forces or insurrectional movements; 8) non-utilization of national territories for aggression against another country; 9) negotiation of matters to do with security, verification, control, and limitation of armaments; 10) urgent attention to refugees and repatriates; 11) cooperation, democracy, and freedom for peace and development; 12) verification and follow-up to the agreements by international bodies.

10 - Contadora and the Support Group, meeting in Sao Paolo, Brazil, call on the international community—especially those countries which have ties with or interests in Central America—to contribute actively to the compliance with the agreements signed by the Central American Presidents so that peace can be attained in the region.

12 - Daniel Ortega invites the Catholic Church and the political parties to form the National Reconciliation Commission (CNR). After the first meeting with Cardinal Obando and 11 political parties, the President reports that the Nicaraguan government has decided to withdraw the suit against Costa Rica in the World Court in order to "contribute to a climate of peace in Central America."

19 - In a press conference, Sergio Ramírez states, "Nicaragua does not have the liquid funds necessary to make cash payments for petroleum purchases." He demands "political and solidarity support" from friendly countries. If this aid is not obtained, he says, "The efforts for peace in Central America could be weakened." The petroleum shortfall for the rest of 1987 is 220,000 metric tons.

20 - Brazilian President José Sarney demands more aid for Nicaragua during a visit to Mexico.

30 - Daniel Ortega announces harsh economic measures and restrictions on fuel consumption. Cargo and inter-urban transport rates are raised. The subsidy to urban transport is maintained. Saturday becomes a workday again in the State apparatus. The gasoline ration quota for private vehicles is reduced from 20 to 17 gallons a month. The elimination of 4,000 vacant jobs in the State is announced.

SEPTEMBER

1 - Robert Dole (U.S. Republican Senator) makes a lightning visit to Nicaragua. Daniel Ortega has a public debate with a group of U.S. Senators. He says: "Leave us Central Americans alone to resolve our problems and don't come here to give us lessons in democracy; we will give them to you." He warned, "The revolution cannot negotiate peace with a pistol at its head." Ortega states that if the United States wants

more freedom and democratization in Nicaragua, it should begin bilateral talks, abide by the ruling of the World Court, and end all forms of support to the mercenaries carrying out the U.S. war of aggression.

2 - The Finance Ministry makes a fiscal reform. Beginning in October, payment of the General Value Tax and income tax will be monthly, not tri-monthly as before, in order to avoid losses in tax values due to inflation. Inflation was 1,342 percent between December 1986 and December 1987. A 7 percent tax on gross monthly sales will be applied. (The previous rate was 20 percent every three months.)

3 - The National Assembly passes the Autonomy Statute for the Regions of the Atlantic Coast.

8 - The USSR responds to the Nicaraguan government's request and announces the delivery of 100,000 metric tons of crude oil in addition to the 300,000 metric tons agreed to previously. It supports the agreements made between the Presidents in Guatemala (Esquipulas II).

9 - MICOIN announces a policy of placing priority on supplies to agricultural workers in order to attract the workforce for the harvest of the agro-export products.

11 - Reagan asks the U.S. Congress for $270 million for the counterrevolution over 18 months.

14 - Daniel Ortega announces the repeal of the Law of Appropriation by the State of abandoned properties, the pardoning of 16 Central Americans captured in counterrevolutionary actions, and the holding of a national dialogue with the legally registered political parties beginning on October 5.

19 - In Managua, the Second Meeting of the Central American Foreign Ministers ends. It is agreed that: 1) each country will commit itself to creating conditions for complying with the Arias Plan; 2) all the Foreign Ministers of Central America and the Verification Commission will be kept informed of the steps that each country is taking; 3) a Commission for Refugees and Displaced People is formed with representatives from all the countries; 4) a sub-committee is set up to study the simultaneity of compliance with the accords dealing with amnesty, cease-fire, democratization, and outside aid to irregular forces.

27 - Daniel Ortega declares a partial amnesty for those who haven't committed atrocities against the Nicaraguan people.

OCTOBER

9 - In a speech delivered to the U.N. General Assembly, Daniel Ortega invites the U.S. President to renew direct and unconditional talks with Nicaragua. It is 35 days after the International Commission for Verification and Follow-up issued its first report about the Esquipulas II Accords.

20 - The Finance Ministry issues an alert about a political campaign organized by COSEP against the economic plan adopted by the government. COSEP had called on producers to not pay the 7 percent tax-in-advance.

NOVEMBER

6 - Daniel Ortega announces the pardoning of 981 prisoners as a gesture of goodwill. The amnesty will be extended and the State of Emergency will be lifted when the International Commission for Verification and Follow-up certifies that the aggression has ended.

8 - Price increases for fuel. For gasoline, the increase is 200 percent.

25 - The first agreement is signed between the government and the political parties in the National Dialogue: 1) proposals for reforms to the Constitution; 2) laws of Municipalities and Political Parties and Electoral Law; 3) municipal elections and elections for the Central American Parliament (PARLACA).

26 - The World Court gives legal recourse to the Nicaraguan suit and authorizes Nicaragua to claim compensation from the United States.

DECEMBER

10 - Comandante Jaime Wheelock reports that an Emergency Committee has been set up to attend to 400,000 people affected by drought. Contingency measures are adopted in order to assure food supply. The bean crop is the most affected.

11 - The new Law of Foreign Investment is enacted.

14 - Adjustment measures are announced. Wages are increased by 100 percent. The lower limit for applying income tax is raised. Subsidies to basic grains will continue.

22 - Contras attack the mining zone in north-central Nicaragua causing heavy losses to and the paralyzing of production in the Bonanza and Rosita mines.

> The U.S. Congress approves $8.1 million for the counterrevolution.

1988

JANUARY

13 - The USSR-Nicaragua Joint Commission meets to sign a three-year agreement for the 1988-1990 period.

15 - A countrywide plan of energy rationing is begun because of problems in getting spare parts for the thermal-electric plants and because of sabotage to a high-tension power pylon near Honduras.

17 - In Costa Rica, the Presidents of Central America agree that the Esquipulas peace process is still in effect and adopt new steps to comply with it.

20 - Reagan says he will ask for whatever is necessary so that the contras "survive." He reactivates his campaign to obtain legal approval of $270 million in contra aid.

24 - The guaranteed price for coffee is adjusted and dollar incentives are maintained.

> Comandante Victor Tirado, in a meeting with UNAG producers, talks of the need to "compact" State-run companies and consolidate cooperatives.

FEBRUARY

1 - Emergency measures to deal with the worsening energy crisis are announced by Vice-president Sergio Ramírez. Priority is given to agricultural production and strategic industrial companies. The workday in the State sector is shortened. This plan is to be in effect for six weeks.

3 - The U.S. Congress rejects (211 for, 219 against) the request for contra funding.

12 - The Ministers of the Economy responsible for Central American economic integration ask the international community for a $1,430 million material aid plan to complement the peace efforts of the Central American governments.

14 - A new turn is made in economic policy. The system of relative prices is corrected. Efficiency and productivity of the economic sectors are sought after. Incentives for exports and rationalization of imports increase the purchasing power of workers.

Monetary reforms are made, including changes of currency. For 1,000 old *córdobas*, 1 new *córdoba* is given. Sums over 10 million *córdobas* per household are frozen for between 12 and 14 months. A new exchange rate is set of ten *córdobas* to the U.S. dollar. New official prices for the products in the basic shopping basket. Salary increases.

19 - The government meets with 200 representatives of all the branches of agricultural production to discuss and agree on new costs and prices for agricultural products.

20 - New austerity measures are announced. Reduction of personnel in the government; budget cutback of 10 percent; not revaluing the 44 million *córdoba* long-term debt of small- and medium-scale ranchers; and rationalization of public investments. A new tax of 55 percent is applied to the profits of the diplo-stores (which sell products in dollars) in order to channel that hard currency into the importation of basic products for the population which will be distributed by means of a network of assured channels.

27 - The "compacting" of different government entities and ministries begins. The Ministries of Industry, Foreign Trade, and Domestic Commerce are fused into the Ministry of Economy, Industry, and Trade with Comandante Luis Carrión as minister. The Ministry of Housing and Human Settlements becomes part of the Ministry of Construction and Transport with Mauricio Valenzuela as minister. The Ministry of Education absorbs the National Council for Higher Education with Fernando Cardenal as minister.

MARCH

1 - The EEC expresses support for the material aid plan for Central America.

3 - The Nicaraguan government designates Defense Minister General Humberto Ortega to hold high-level talks with the counterrevolution, directly and without intermediaries, in Nicaraguan territory in order to attain a cease-fire. At the same time in the United States, a call is made in the U.S. Congress for "humanitarian assistance" for the contras.

MICOIN announces free commerce in basic grains and ends the roadblocks after a self-critical review of their effectiveness: they encouraged hoarding.

11 - New limits for financing are set for commercial banks. The bank will finance 80 percent of the operating costs of agriculture and the remaining 20 percent will be assumed by the producers. For livestock breeding and fattening, the limit is 70 percent. On March 4, 1988, it is announced that the official exchange rate will be devalued periodically.

13 - Incentives and guaranteed prices for coffee and cotton are adjusted.

16 - A "compacting" of the sugar sector is announced. The Sugar Corporation is created. It has a joint State-private sector character. It will encourage greater efficiency and take actions to confront the blockade.

18 - The banks announce new interest rates.

24 - The first cease-fire agreement with the counterrevolution is signed at Sapoá.

28 - The first 100 amnestied prisoners leave jail.

APRIL

11 - The National Fisheries Corporation is created.

23 - The Sébaco Valley agro-industrial complex is opened.

MAY

12 - The United Nations approves a $4370 million Special Plan of Economic Cooperation for Central America.

13 - Some workers demand a dynamic wage policy in order to hold back the deterioration of their salaries.

JUNE

14 - New measures are announced. Freeing up of prices and wages in line with costs and profitability of the companies, except for the wages of those in the State sector. Periodic indexation of the exchange rate and the savings and lending interest rates. New exchange rate of 80 *córdobas* to the U.S. dollar (700 percent devaluation). 1,000 percent increase in fuel prices. Salary increase of 30 percent in the State sector. More space to be given to market forces in order to correct imbalances in relative prices and to encourage efficiency and productivity. New policy of incentives for agro-exports: dollar incentives are maintained for meat, cotton, and coffee plus a 25 percent reward on top of the value of production when it is over the average for the last three-year period. For exporters of non-traditional products, 50 percent will be paid in dollars that come from exports, and in the case of industry, it will be 25 percent. Policy of indexation of interest rates in order to reduce financial losses to the banks.

19 - Payment for zoning and seniority given to workers in education and health care instituted as ways to compensate for low nominal salaries.

29 - The National Assembly passes the Law of Municipalities. It sets the basis for holding municipal elections and regulates municipal activity.

JULY

6 - The sale at subsidized prices of a food package (AFA) is announced. It will contain ten pounds each of rice and beans and five pounds of sugar for all State-sector workers. Workers with low salaries are to pay 5 percent of their base wage and the rest will pay 10 percent. In the first stage, the AFA will go to 92,000 workers.

7 - The People's Commercial Corporation (CORCOP) announces that it will limit its profit margin to 10 percent in order to offer basic goods at lower prices. In general, sales are greatly contracted.

12 - The Nicaraguan government expels U.S. ambassador Richard Melton and seven other U.S. embassy officials for involvement in the domestic affairs of Nicaragua. The next day, in reprisal, the U.S. government gives 72 hours to Nicaragua's representative to the OAS, Carlos Tünnermann, and seven officials of Nicaragua's diplomatic mission in Washington for them to leave the country.

13 - The San Antonio sugar refinery and all properties belonging to Nicaragua Sugar Estates Limited, property of the Pellas family, are declared to be a public utility of social interest by MIDINRA. The State intervention is based on the abandonment and deterioration of the installations and a drop in production.

31 - Reagan asks the U.S. Congress to support the bill presented by Robert Dole for $27 million in "humanitarian assistance" to the counterrevolution and another $20 million in military aid. On August 11, 1988, the U.S. Senate approves the $27 million in humanitarian assistance and $16 million in military aid (49 for, 47 against).

AUGUST

4 - The Central Bank of Nicaragua announces a new system of indexing interest rates on loans. Rates are monthly and cumulative for each loan and disbursement. Preferential rates for cooperatives are eliminated. However, after the damages later caused by Hurricane Joan, in December 1988, it will be decided to made credit more flexible, fixing a rate equivalent to half the normal rate for agriculture for the growing season and 100 percent of the operating costs will be financed.

The government reports that the World Court sentence was rejected by the United States and it urges the United States to abide by the ruling and the demand for compensation for damages caused by the aggression.

6 - U.N.ICEF praises the National Campaign for the Defense of the Life of the Child promoted by the Nicaraguan government and begun on this date under the presidency of Daniel Ortega.

19 - The corn crop for this growing season is a record for the last ten years.

24 - The ATC accuses producers linked to COSEP of not complying with collective agreements.

25 - The National Assembly passes the Electoral Law.

29 - Fuel prices are raised.

31 - Devaluation from 80 *córdobas* to the U.S. dollar to 180 to 1. A salary increase of 140 percent beginning in September is announced for all State-sector workers.

SEPTEMBER

1 - The Ministry of Economy, Industry, and Commerce (MEIC) announces a new system of payment to coffee producers. The guaranteed price is suppressed and producers are given the international price on the basis of the average sale price to ENCAFE. Dollar incentives are maintained.

5 - A special salary for the countryside is set in order to guarantee labor stability. The agro-export harvest is given priority.

26 - Revaluation of the fixed shares in companies. Tax on profits will not exceed 50 percent. For agricultural activities, the rate is 40 percent, 45 percent for industry, and 50 percent for commercial and service activities. Prior to this, the ceiling had been 60 percent.

OCTOBER

21 - Hurricane Joan blows through Nicaragua. 186,950 people affected, 29,152 homes destroyed, 66 bridges washed away. The CEPAL estimates damages to be $840 million. 500,000 hectares of sub-tropical rainforest are blown down.

NOVEMBER

8 - A 78 percent wage increase is given to State-sector workers. Interest rates are reduced for 60,000 campesino families affected by the hurricane.

11 - The Minister of Tourism, Herty Lewites, reports that contacts have been made with Nicaraguan private investors in order to offer them shares in some tourism complexes.

20 - The National Coffee Commission is formed.

DECEMBER

15 - The National Cotton Commission approves a new mechanism for paying producers on the basis of the average sale price on the international market.

19 - Part of the profits generated by the diplo-store (domestic sales in dollars) are used by the government to import toys which will be given out to 300,000 Nicaraguan children.

21 - The lack of money in circulation provokes a reduction in the rate for the dollar on the black market. The money-changing houses also reduce their rate.

1989

JANUARY

16 - The President and the National Planning Council (CNP) meet with rural workers to analyze the economic situation and propose alternatives. 1) The selective recovery of production of products for basic consumption and export is proposed as well as an overall plan for transferring the workforce from the city to the countryside. 2) It is proposed that adjustments to the expenditures made by the State-sector not affect workers' wages. The commitment is made to relocate those affected.

21 - Electricity rates rise by 106 percent.

25 - The official exchange rate goes from 2,000 to 2,300 *córdobas* to the U.S. dollar.

27 - Cotton growers say they are in favor of *concertación* (or social pact) in order to help overcome the economic situation and they ask the government to take action in order to ensure the cotton harvest.

29 - New adjustments are made to the prices charged for fiscal products and fuel.

30 - The government and the Pellas family reach an agreement on compensation for declaring the San Antonio sugar refinery a public utility.

FEBRUARY

2 - The Vice-minister of MIDINRA announces that there will be no more land confiscations. He says that *latifundismo* (ownership of large tracts of land) has been reduced from 36 percent to 9 percent of the arable land, benefitting 120,000 campesino families with the distribution of 3,000,000 *manzanas* (1 *manzana* = 1.73 acres).

The director of ENABAS announces the reduction in the number of products that that agency distributes from more than 100 basic products to 16 in order to allow for the development of non-monopoly commerce.

6 - The Finance Ministry announces the application of drastic measures in order to ensure greater tax revenues and reduce the fiscal deficit.

7 - The government announces incentives for the producers of basic grains, authorizing the export of these products. Debts are restructured and the necessary financing is provided in order to guarantee the production goals set for this growing season.

Taxes are raised to 50 percent on the profits of APP companies involved in commerce and in the industry of fiscal products.

8 - The Central Bank of Nicaragua announces the free sale of dollars to priority sectors in the money-changing houses.

10 - The Interior Ministry announces measures in order to reduce its expenditures. Personnel are dismissed and migration offices are closed in the regions.

13 - New bank interest rates are announced.

14 - Daniel Ortega reports on the decision to advance the elections to the first trimester of 1990.

15 - The Presidents of Central America, meeting in El Salvador, agree to draw up in less than 90 days a joint plan for the demobilization, repatriation, or voluntary relocation in Nicaragua or third countries of the members of the Nicaraguan Resistance and their relatives. The technical advice of specialized bodies of the United Nations is asked for.

23 - The official exchange rate is devalued to 3,800 *córdobas* to the U.S. dollar and fuel prices are adjusted accordingly.

MARCH

4 - The banks make their financing policy more flexible: 100 percent for the purchase of agro-chemical inputs, 70 percent for labor costs. Financing of 100 percent is authorized for the financeable costs of cotton producers so that they can have yields above the break-even point. Long-term preferential credit is granted to coffee and livestock producers.

8 - A Japanese technical mission arrives to carry out preliminary studies for the construction of an inter-oceanic canal through Nicaragua.

The National Planning Council approves measures in order to encourage the planting of basic grains. The program includes pricing, purchase, and credit policies.

9 - Daniel Ortega announces a program to supply milk to schoolchildren.

10 - Daniel Ortega announces a lowering of interest rates for credit and 100 percent financing of the livestock sector.

15 - The National Assembly approves the President's request to pardon 932 former National Guardsmen.

30 - The official exchange rate is devalued and fuel prices are adjusted.

31 - The Health Ministry announces a plan to decentralize units and municipalize health services.

APRIL

1 - The reduction in the consumer price index allows for a lowering of interest rates. A tax is placed on sales in the diplo-stores. Diplomats are exempted.

13 - The exchange rate is devalued to 6,500 *córdobas* to the U.S. dollar.

14 - The U.S. House of Representatives approves (309 for, 110 against) $49.7 million in "humanitarian assistance" for the contras and collateral assignations to other sectors for a total of $60 million.

21 - Daniel Ortega and the CNP, in a meeting with agricultural producers, agree to adopt measures to encourage production: 1) monthly interest rates of no more than 20 percent are set. They can be reviewed every four months; 2) respect of private property and the creation of a land bank: 3) cancelation and restructuring of campesino debts; 4) subsidy to cotton production; 5) incentives for the production of coffee and meat; 6) guaranteed prices for basic grains; 7) support to the rice, poultry, and pork sectors.

23 - Daniel Ortega calls on his Central American counterparts to comply with the commitments assumed in Costa del Sol, El Salvador and to make a recount of those complied with by Nicaragua. He also condemns the opposition groups which made a pact in Guatemala to continue the war.

30 - First Vice-president of Sweden, Ingvar Carlsson, tells President Ortega in Stockholm that Sweden has decided to increase the amount of yearly aid by 40 million Swedish crowns for a total of 230 million. He also expressed interest in being the host country for an international meeting about the economic development of Nicaragua to be held in Sweden on May 11 and 12.

MAY

4 - Sergio Ramírez announces that the monthly inflation rate has dropped and so interest rates for the month of May are lowered. The price of diesel and lubricants goes down by 30 percent and the charge for electricity for irrigation is lowered by 15 percent. These were things requested by producers in the April 21 meeting.

12 - In Stockholm, the first Conference of Donor Countries ends. It is agreed to immediately grant Nicaragua $50 million and credit lines for the purchase of equipment and inputs for production.

Ramiro Gurdian, a COSEP leader, announces that milk producer Juan Diego López has been expelled from that organization for having participated in the conference in Stockholm.

20 - In Harare, Zimbabwe, the Foreign Ministers of the Non-Aligned Nations agree to give full support to the Costa del Sol accords and say that the steps taken by Nicaragua in compliance with the agreements are an effective contribution to peace and regional stability. They call on all sides to comply equally with the letter and spirit of that which was agreed.

21 - A division occurs in COSEP's ranks. FONDILAC (representing milk producers) leaves because of pressures to act against the interests of producers.

26 - The Nicaraguan government decides to expel two functionaries of the U.S. embassy in Managua for involvement in domestic political affairs. On June 1, the United States gives 72 hours for the advisory ministers to the Nicaraguan embassy in Washington to leave the country in reprisal for Nicaragua's action.

31 - The exchange rate goes to 8,300 *córdobas* to the U.S. dollar. Inflation, which had dropped to 12.5 percent in April, went up again in May to 15.5 percent.

JUNE

1 - The President, in a meeting with education workers, announces a 14 percent wage increase, the decentralization of the teaching profession, and the creation of a social fund made up of contributions from the APP companies in order to compensate for the decline in teachers' salaries. Payments for working in different zones and for seniority are increased from 25 percent to 40 percent of the base salary and a commitment is made to work on job reclassifications.

7 - New incentives are announced for cotton production: 50 percent of the earnings will be paid in dollars, plus an additional $10 per hundredweight for those who produce over 35 hundredweight per *manzana* (1.73 acres).

8 - Alfredo César arrives in Nicaragua under the Amnesty Law.

13 - Daniel Ortega calls producers together and announces a series of new measures: 50 percent salary increase for education and health workers and 36 percent for the rest of the State sector; 114 percent devaluation and changes in interest rates; subsidies for the consumption of cooking gas, kerosene, and diesel; fiscal spending remains reduced; the investment plan is cut back but remains steady for road maintenance; the parallel money market is freed of controls; prices are adjusted for basic grains.

15 - ENABAS announces a price freeze on basic grains for the rest of the month of June.

16 - The MEIC orients companies to reduce profit margins in order to avoid an elevated increase in prices.

17 - A U.S. congressional commission approves $3 million to be distributed to the OAS and the National Endowment for Democracy (NED) to be used for "the work of observation in Nicaragua." A plan known about earlier was for the NED to earmark these funds for the activities of the Nicaraguan opposition in the upcoming election campaign.

19 - In Matagalpa, a meeting of coffee growers affiliated with COSEP is held. The leaders try to have a five-point communiqué issued but it is rejected by the majority of the producers present. It was to announce withdrawal from the National Coffee Commission. Nicolás Bolaños Gayer announces that there is a program for a government of "national salvation."

21 - The U.S. State Department rejects Nicaragua's proposal to begin contacts between the two countries and conditions it on compliance with "certain conditions such as there being free elections."

22 - The Nicaraguan government announces the expropriation of the properties of COSEP leaders Jaime Cuadra, Nicolás Bolaños, and Arnoldo Alemán in response to the "open attitude of confrontation of these people against the process of economic *concertación* which the government is carrying out with the producers."

26 - President Daniel Ortega announces that the official exchange rate will remain stable for the months of June and July.

The government, in a meeting with representatives of small- and medium-sized industries, announces the exoneration from tax payments for two years. 100 percent of the import duty on machinery for industry is exonerated and 40 percent on imports of tools and spare parts for the industrial sector.

27 - The Vice-president of the Central Bank of Nicaragua reports that on the parallel market the price of the dollar has dropped from 26,250 *córdobas* to 25,750.

An extraordinary meeting of the National Coffee Commission is called to look at different aspects of coffee cultivation. The producers ask for interest rates on deposits in banks for payments for last year's crop to be reviewed. 50 percent of the savings interest is due. They want the time to be extended for the presentation of investment plans and the return of 40 percent of the tax revenues collected from them by the Finance Ministry.

30 - The U.S. House of Representatives approves a measure to allow the government to provide covert aid to the political parties loyal to U.S. policy (Hyde amendment: 298 for, 118 against).

JULY

4 - The Nicaraguan government announces the exoneration of import duties on passenger transport vehicles and the sale of 406 trucks at favorable terms to private carriers.

5 - The National Reconciliation Commission (CNR) reports that consensus has been achieved: "The Nicaraguan government has taken steps in compliance with the Costa del Sol agreements." It says, "There should be a voluntary demobilization of the counterrevolution stationed in Honduras and these steps should continue in order to end on February 25, 1990."

8 - The first U.N. mission to observe the electoral process arrives in Managua.

14 - Judge Roettget of the Federal Court of Fort Lauderdale, Florida hands down a final verdict that the United States, in effect, has taken warlike actions against Nicaragua.

AUGUST

3 - The National Dialogue begins; 21 legally registered political parties participate.

8 - The Central American presidential summit meeting in Tela, Honduras ends. A period of three months is set for the dismantling of the counterrevolutionary bases in Honduras, after the International Commission for Support and Verification (CIAV) is set up.

16 - The *córdoba* is devalued to 20,600 to the U.S. dollar.

The first 29 from a list presented by UNAG of 1,200 campesinos detained for counterrevolutionary activities are freed.

17 - The Finance Ministry announces a reduction of the taxes applied to 90 industrial products in order to favor the reactivation of the industrial sector which had been building up inventories due to a lack of sales.

24 - The *córdoba* is devalued to 21,300 to the U.S. dollar.

SEPTEMBER

3 - The political parties in the UNO coalition nominate Violeta Chamorro as their presidential candidate and Virgilio Godoy as their vice-presidential candidate. Godoy is openly opposed by COSEP.

4 - Authorities of the Central Bank say the stability experienced by the money-changing houses allows for a more open policy for the buying and selling of dollars. Such operations are authorized to be conducted at commercial bank branches in all regions of the country.

8 - Powdered milk is to be distributed to all State-sector employees. It is also announced that 100,000 school-children will be covered by the daily glass of milk program.

9 - The *córdoba* is devalued to 22,000 to the U.S. dollar.

17 - Jimmy Carter arrives in Managua as the coordinator of the Movement of Freely Elected Presidents.

21 - The FSLN nominates Daniel Ortega as its presidential candidate and Sergio Ramírez as its vice-presidential candidate.

According to inside sources, Bush asks the U.S. Congress for $9 million in direct and indirect aid for the campaign of Violeta Chamorro.

23 - A 30 percent salary increase, to be applied in steps, is announced. In October, education workers will receive it, in November, health workers, and in December, the remaining State-sector employees.

29 - Daniel Ortega announces a series of economic measures to benefit 5,000 war wounded. These include a social fund and a housing program.

OCTOBER

3 - Interest rates are lowered again. Education and health workers receive a 30 percent wage increase. The rest of the public sector gets 15 percent.

DECEMBER

13 - The Central American presidential summit meeting in San Isidro de Coronado, Costa Rica ends. It is agreed to: condemn the actions of irregular forces in the region; ask the counterrevolution to demobilize immediately; respect human rights in Central America; and find a negotiated solution to the conflict in El Salvador. Support is expressed for the idea that the funds approved by the United States for the counterrevolution be channeled by the CIAV for the repatriation and demobilization of Nicaraguan Resistance members in Honduras.

20 - U.S. troops invade Panama.

22 - Foreign Minister Miguel D'Escoto reports that the U.S. embassy in Nicaragua is surrounded by tanks, armored cars, and artillery in response to the U.S. action of surrounding the Nicaraguan embassy in Panama.

1990

JANUARY

9 - In an extraordinary session of the OAS Permanent Council, a resolution is passed by a wide margin to declare the search conducted by the U.S. Armed Forces of the residence of the Nicaraguan ambassador in Panama illegal.

10 - Daniel Ortega announces the creation of a $500,000 and 10 million *córdoba* cash fund to finance 3,000 craft workshops and small industries in Masaya, Granada, and Carazo. The restructuring of that sector's 20 million *córdoba* debt to the SFN is also announced, along with preferential interest rates and the cancelation of tax debts to the Finance Ministry. Income taxes are exonerated for one year.

22 - The *córdoba* is devalued to 46,380 to the U.S. dollar, but this time the prices of cooking gas, diesel, gasoline, and transport rates are not raised accordingly.

26 - The government announces measures to help campesinos: reduction of agricultural retentions, restructuring of bank debts, Law to Create the

Fund for Development of Cooperatives, and exoneration from tax payments for cooperatives affected by the war.

FEBRUARY

8 - The National Assembly approves the pardon requested by the President of 39 former members of the National Guard and campesino collaborators of the counterrevolution.

20 - The presidents of the Chambers of Industry and Commerce, Jaime Bengoechea and L. López Zeledón, agree that it is important to work more closely with the Sandinista government after the elections and they say they are willing to discuss a new relation between private enterprise and the State.

21 - More than 600,000 people attend the final campaign rally of the FSLN in Managua.

22 - The accounts of the Nicaraguan government in Panamanian banks are frozen on orders from the U.S. Southern Command.

24 - A number of high-level Bush administration functionaries express the opinion that a free and fair victory by Daniel Ortega would oblige the United States to normalize relations with Nicaragua.

25 - Elections are held in Nicaragua. The final results give 55 percent to the UNO and 41 percent to the FSLN.

26 - At 6 a.m., Daniel Ortega speaks to the nation and announces that "the President of Nicaragua and the government are going to respect and abide by the popular mandate expressed in the election vote." He considers that "to guarantee a pure electoral process which will encourage our consciences even more towards the consolidation of democracy, a mixed economy, liberty, and the independence of the country without intervention by an outside power is, at this historical moment, the main contribution that Sandinistas are giving to the people of Nicaragua."

MARCH

3 - The Presidents of Central America end a summit meeting at Montelimar, Nicaragua and ask for the immediate demobilization and disarmament of the counterrevolutionaries who are inside or outside of Nicaragua by April 25, 1990 at the latest. They call for compliance with the agreements signed at Tela (August 1989) and at Toncontín. The weapons are to be destroyed *in situ* by ONUCA, the U.N. peace-keeping mission.

13 - Bush offers to lift the embargo against Nicaragua and asks the U.S. Congress for $500 million in aid, $300 million of which is to be disbursed in the short term.

20 - A mission of the new government travels to Japan in order to obtain emergency aid. Japan gives $2 million worth of fertilizer.

22 - A delegation from the United States presided over by the Under-secretary of State for Latin American Affairs arrives in Managua. In the group are functionaries of the U.S. State Department, the Treasury Department, and the AID.

25 - Daniel Ortega announces a restructuring and cancelation of the debts of cotton growers, basic grains producers, and cooperatives affected by the bad rainy season. The payments owed for the purchase of agricultural equipment are also cancelled.

27 - The Transition Teams of President Daniel Ortega and President-elect Violeta Chamorro sign an accord after one month of discussions. They agree on, among other things: 1) the immediate demobilization of the counterrevolution; 2) subordination of the Armed Forces and the domestic security forces to the civilian power of the President; 3) guaranteeing ownership of the urban and rural properties given out by the State prior to February 25, 1990.

APRIL

10 - The *córdoba* is devalued to 51,200 to the U.S. dollar. A salary increase is declared for the month of April, setting the minimum wage at 50 percent of the price of a 53-item shopping basket of basic goods. The government announces the cancelation of the debts of taxi drivers, producers, and transporters for the vehicles included in the special programs of 1989-90.

21 - Daniel Ortega speaks at the closing of the National Assembly elected in 1984. Dr. Miriam Argüello is named as President of the new National Assembly.

25 - Violeta Barrios de Chamorro is sworn in as President. The new Cabinet is sworn in. It has 12 Ministers of State and 7 ministers of autonomous entities.

26 - The government announces a 100 percent devaluation of the parallel money market exchange rate. It is now 140,000 córdobas to the U.S. dollar.

27 - The official exchange rate is devalued by 23 percent to 70,000 to the U.S. dollar. Devaluations occur on an average of twice weekly until July, and then once a week from August on.

MAY

3 - The government authorizes increases in the prices of transport, liquors, meat, and milk. This policy continues in the following months.

4 - The President of the Central Bank of Nicaragua announces the decision by the Executive Council to introduce a new series of bills and coins which will be on a par with the U.S. dollar. It will be called the "córdoba oro."

5 - The Ministry of Labor announces the suspension of the AFA, alleging that it is a wage subterfuge.

8 - The Nicaraguan Workers Front (FNT) is formed by seven unions with more than 200,000 members. It declares itself to be against the government proposal to increase wages by 60 percent and asks for an audience with the President to discuss the problems faced by workers.

9 - Violeta Chamorro delegates the Minister of Labor to negotiate with the workers. Because of a stagnation of negotiations, the FNT declares a strike which is to be extended in stages.

The government announces the suspension of the Law of Civil Service and the transportation subsidy for students.

10 - A strike breaks out in the State sector.

11 - The Executive Power promulgates Decrees Nos. 10-90 and 11-90 dealing with the Provisional Leasing of (State-owned) Lands and the Review of Confiscations.

12 - Daniel Ortega calls on the government to reflect and be coherent with its discourse about reconciliation, and demands "to leave without effect the latest decrees which are an attempt to kill the democratic conquests in the political, economic, and social planes."

15 - The Minister of Labor breaks off talks with the workers and declares the strike to be "illegal, illicit, and non-existent." He threatens massive firings and the use of public force in order to evict workers from the government installations which they occupied peacefully.

17 - The government and the FNT reach agreements. The strike ends. The agreements are: 1) 25 percent salary increase over April wages; 2) a salary increase in June based on the increase in the cost of the 53-item shopping basket; 3) respect for the collective agreements signed by the teachers' union (ANDEN) and the health workers' federation (FETSALUD); 4) review with workers' participation of the collective agreements signed between February 25 and April 25; 5) regulation of Law of Civil Service; 6) no reprisals against strikers.

20 - The FNT denounces the government implementation of unconstitutional measures and wants to introduce reforms to the Law of Civil Service which would in effect mean its repeal.

23 - The agreements between the FNT and the government are violated. Massive firings are announced in the Ministries of Labor, Construction and Transport, and Foreign Affairs.

28 - Extraofficially, it is reported that the Consumer Price Index for the month of May rose by more than 100 percent.

The Executive Power promulgates Decree 1-90, which goes against the attributions conferred by the Constitution on the State Powers, violating their independence.

30 - The National Assembly passes the Law of University Autonomy. The amendments suggested by the Executive Power are not included.

JUNE

2 - The FNT and the government agree on: a 65 percent salary increase; the delivery of the AFA corresponding to May and June; an increase in the lower limit for application of income taxes; a correction of salaries less than 15 million *córdobas*; and a fresh review of salaries on June 30.

6 and **7** - The second Conference of Donor Countries is held in Rome with the participation of Sergio Ramírez on behalf of the opposition.

9 - Venezuela announces that it will supply petroleum again.

The government announces that electricity rates will be charged in "*córdobas oro*", the new currency pegged to the U.S. dollar. On June 15, water rates are indexed similarly.

17 - The FSLN agrees to hold its first party congress in February 1991. (This date was later changed to July 1991.)

29 - The government announces the "dollarization" of payments for all taxes and makes new adjustments to tax rates.

JULY

2 - A strike by 50,000 State-sector workers begins. It is motivated by the economic situation and by the attempts to roll back conquests of the revolution. Workers ask to discuss the Economic Program and demand an end to the process of privatizing the APP. The strike grows in the following days.

4 - The main FNT leaders are detained by police for a few hours.

5 - Negotiations break off between the FNT and the government. The strike gains force and takes on an almost insurrectional character. Some confrontations happen.

12 - President Violeta Chamorro commits herself to begin a National Dialogue in order to arrive at a "social agreement." The negotiation commission reaches an agreement and the strike ends.

14 - The FNT denounces a wave of firings in the State sector.

23 - COSEP businesspeople question the government's economic policy.

25 - Producers ask the government for policies with preferential financial treatment to help the production of coffee, cotton, and meat. They also ask to be paid for the last crop.

31 - The FNT denounces the government for not complying with its agreements and warns that it won't attend the National Dialogue if the agreements continue to be broken.

AUGUST

5 - Diplomatic sources reveal that U.S. Ambassador to Nicaragua, Harry Schlaudeman, personally and in the name of the Bush administration, demanded to the Ministry of Foreign Affairs that Nicaragua drop its suit against the U.S. government in the World Court.

10 - The Office of the Attorney General resolves to return the Borden Chemical company—taken over by the State in 1983—to its former owners.

14 - Minister of the Presidency Antonio Lacayo, in a press conference, acknowledges that the "Mayorga plan" was "no more than a collection of ideas of a macroeconomic order." However, the seriousness of the crisis "made it necessary to think about the economy in a much more serious manner than had been done during the transition."

17 - Violeta Chamorro asks the National Assembly to pardon the murderers of Pedro Joaquín Chamorro.

22 - The National Assembly rejects (30 for, 51 against) the bill for a pardon of Chamorro's murderers, pointing out that this is "in defense of the security and stability of Nicaraguans."

24 - The National Employees Union (UNE) says it is in the process of organizing 1,391 workers that have joined the ranks of the unemployed since the change of government.

27 - Finance Minister Emilio Pereira announces a new tax reform law meant to control inflation and reduce public spending. The law exonerates taxes on imported products and consumer goods.

The FSLN electoral committee announces that some 20,000 Sandinista militants took part in the party's electoral process in Managua, in which new district and municipal authorities were chosen.

29 - UNE Secretary-general José Angel Bermúdez denounces government plans to fire 12,000 State workers, including 4,000 soldiers.

Five UNO deputies introduce a bill to eliminate all the names of "heroes and martyrs" from national parks, plazas, public buildings, and monuments, despite agreements in the Transition Protocol to respect the names.

31 - Workers from the National Financial System begin partial strikes in different banks of the country to protest the refusal of banking authorities to negotiate salaries and job security. They demand a 145 percent salary increase.

In a debate sponsored by the National Autonomous University of Nicaragua (UNAN) called "A Possible Nicaragua," former President Daniel Ortega demands concrete acts by the government to create the necessary climate for *concertación*. Minister of the Presidency Antonio Lacayo says *concertación* cannot proceed while the problem of hyperinflation remains unresolved.

SEPTEMBER

8 - COSEP President Gilberto Cuadra says his organization and U.S. Ambassador Harry Schlaudeman agree completely that privatization of all State businesses is an indispensible prerequisite for foreign economic aid to the new government.

Former contras in Matagalpa threaten to intensify their pressures to receive land, going from taking over State farms (UPEs) to more violent actions such as blocking transport, communication, and access to certain towns.

9 - The Association of Workers of the Countryside (ATC) issues a communiqué denouncing the climate of repression in the countryside caused by government Decrees 10-90 and 11-90, and demands the legalization of businesses in the name of the workers, warning that it will not permit the dismemberment of any State Production Units (UPEs).

Vice-minister of Foreign Cooperation Noel Vidaure says the U.S. Agency for International Development (AID) is holding back on $260 million of the $300 million promised by the United States for Nicaragua.

Former contra leader Oscar "Rubén" Sovalbarro accuses Israel "Franklyn" Galeano of accepting bribes from Sandinistas and government officials.

10 - Daniel Ortega asks European countries to send economic aid to Nicaragua while on a tour of West Germany, Italy, and Sweden.

2,000 campesinos and workers take to the streets in Matagalpa to protest hunger, poverty, and social and economic instability caused by government policies.

11 - After meeting with Daniel Ortega, officials of the West German government announce a donation of some $16 million in immediate aid for Nicaragua.

12 - The President of the political party of former contras, "Rubén", claims the nearly 20,000 former contras need some 500,000 *manzanas* of land to survive (1 *manzana* = 1.73 acres).

Workers from SOVIPE Construction, DELMOR (canned food) Industries, Prego Soaps, El Caracol Coffee, and Luna Beds warn that they are ready to take over the businesses if the government decides they are to be privatized.

13 - The FSLN National Directorate issues a communiqué calling on the government to "create the minimum conditions" for *concertación*. Reading the official message, Comandante Luis Carrión says the country is in a truly explosive condition.

14 - President Chamorro announces the official opening of the process of *concertación*, calling on the different national sectors to meet in Managua on September 20.

15 - Enrique Chavarría, a Managua judge, says the crime rate in the capital has risen by 80 percent since April.

17 - The FNT says it will not participate in the process of *concertación* so long as the government does not respect the accords signed on July 12.

The FSLN National Directorate issues a communiqué demanding that the government postpone for 30 days the start of the program of *concertación* so that it has time to create the necessary climate of confidence.

The official exchange rate is devalued to 1,120,000 cìrdobas to the dollar. The black market rate hits 1,300,000 to one. Devaluations continue to occur every Monday. The black market consistently remains slightly above the official.

18 - President Chamorro rejects the FSLN's request to postpone the *concertación* process.

19 - Minister of the Presidency Antonio Lacayo signs an agreement with U.S. ambassador Schlaudeman and AID Director Janet Ballantyne. $10 million will be used immediately to stimulate employment.

20 - Opening the process of *concertación*, President Chamorro says, "Our goal is to achieve certain accords between the producers, workers, and government that will allow the social and economic costs of stabilizing the country to be reduced."

Unions of the FNT (CST, ATC, UNE, ANDEN, and FETSALUD) announce a process of "generalized resistance" in response to government measures. Some 5,000 workers demonstrate outside the convention center where the *concertación* meeting is being held.

22 - Leaders of the former contra group ARDE/Southern Front send a letter to President Chamorro saying they will "take political action to discredit her" if she continues to ignore the commitments made in accords signed in El Almendro on June 12.
25 - Sixteen State-owned firms are returned to their former owners by the government. A *Barricada* editorial calls it the government's "social counterrevolution." Workers at two of the firms (El Caracol coffee and Luna Beds) occupy their workplaces.
26 - In a signing ceremony in New York, Nicaragua receives $118 million, $68 million to pay for petroleum over the next six months, and $50 million to make payments on the debt to the World Bank.
27 - Daniel Ortega meets with Antonio Lacayo, U.S. Ambassador Schlaudeman, and U.N. Representative to Nicaragua Francesco Vicenti at the U.N. offices. They talk about the possibility of drawing up an economic program of consensus which would also be acceptable to the IMF.
28 - Chamorro meets with George Bush in New York and asks for $200 million annually for at least four years, a fund for privatization projects, and a friendship and cooperation treaty.
29 - The pro-government construction workers union SCAAS demands a minimum wage of $500 a month.

OCTOBER

2 - Venezuela offers Nicaragua and the other countries of Central America a 50 percent rebate on petroleum payments if these are made at the time of purchase.
4 - The second meeting of the *concertación* process is held. The Sandinista organizations demand two delegates for each sector represented, but they settle for one. An executive committee is formed with two representatives each from government, business, and labor. *Barricada* calls it "real *concertación*."
5 - Attorney General Dulio Baltodano says there are 3,500 files open to review confiscations made during the Sandinista administration.

Sergio Ramírez says the FSLN will respect any agreement reached in the *concertación* process and make its membership comply with it. He expresses optimism about the process.
9 - The Agrarian Reform Institute (INRA) issues a report about land problems. 400 former contras have occupied a number of farms and three cooperatives in Region V (Boaco, Chontales). In Jinotega, campesinos from a co-op have occupied the INRA offices protesting the invasion of their lands. Some farms near Matagalpa have been taken over by members of the ATC. In both regions, INRA has distributed 84,287 *manzanas* (1 *manzana* = 1.73 acres) to former contras and repatriates.

Labor Minister Francisco Rosales presents a proposal for a freeze on wages and prices, elimination of the AFA food subsidy package, and elimination of overtime pay and other subsidies. It is rejected by the FNT delegates.

According to *Time* magazine, some U.S. government officials are considering a freeze on aid to Nicaragua until it drops the suit in the World Court.

An agreement is signed with Japan for that country to donate $3.7 million towards the purchase of agricultural equipment.

10 - President Chamorro asks the members of the Economic Cabinet to hand in their resignations in preparation for a Cabinet shuffle.

11 - The National Assembly unanimously approves a nine-point declaration dealing with *concertación*. Among other things, the document states that the elected government must be allowed to implement its program and the representation of the opposition must be considered in the decisions made by the government.

Vice-minister of Foreign Affairs Vidaurre denies that U.S. government officials are arguing that Nicaragua should not receive aid unless it drops its suit at the Hague. Daniel Ortega says that the government should press the World Court to rule on the exact amount of damages that Nicaragua should receive in reparations.

Members of the Chamber of Commerce ask where the $60 million of AID money is that was earmarked to promote the business sector. Apparently, $20 million went to cover "other needs of the State," including payments for petroleum.

14 - It is reported that school textbooks for which the paper was donated by Norway will be burned because they reflect the "leftist" stance of the Sandinista government. Vice-minister of Education Humberto Belli says the texts have a "highly political content." The other Vice-minister says some texts have "very daring" sections about sexual education.

16 - Because the cost of a barrel of oil from Venezuela has gone up to $36.02, the price of a gallon of gasoline is raised to 2.35 *cìrdobas oro*, a 9.3 percent increase.

The FNT says it will return to the *concertación* talks in order to continue fighting for the government to adopt a plan which takes workers' demands into account. Union leader Lucio Jiménez says, "If the government insists on imposing its plan, that's where *concertación* stops and all that would be left for the workers is to definitively leave the [talks] and go and resist in the streets."

17 - President Chamorro travels to Venezuela to visit President Carlos Andres Pérez and ask for emergency aid. On her return, she announces that trade debts of $14 million and $150 million have been renegotiated to be paid over 40 years and that 15,000 barrels of oil a day until the end of 1991 are guaranteed.

Demobilized contras take over privately owned land near San Juan del Río Coco. They are supported by campesinos on nearby cooperatives.

18 - Colonel Hugo Torres says that between 4,500 and 5,000 officers will be discharged as part of the first phase of a reduction of the armed forces.

In the *concertación* forum, the FNT proposal is presented and is strongly attacked by other participants, in particular COSEP representatives. Ramiro Gurdian of COSEP also criticizes the government for being too weak in dealing with the Sandinistas, whom he calls "thieves and criminals." He says, "Either the government puts on the pants or says that it can't govern the country in order to see if we can do it." The FNT accuses him of promoting a coup.

23 - In a press conference, the FSLN National Directorate issues a statement calling for the signing of a *concertación* agreement "immediately." Daniel Ortega says that either there is an agreement or there isn't, but it has be resolved this week.

24 - Poll results released by the Institute for Nicaraguan Studies (IEN) say that 58 percent of those polled feel that since the UNO government took office the economic situation has worsened; 61.2 percent feel health and education services have declined; 78 percent believe that unemployment has gone up; 56.8 percent feel that the government hasn't kept its election promises; 89.2 percent are against freezing public sector salaries; 87.2 percent reject the government plan to dismiss 15,000 workers; and 92.4 percent agree that it is necessary to finance the productive sector.

25 - Canada signs an agreement with Nicaragua to provide a $15 million credit line.

The electric company (INE) says that more than half its 300,000 customers are in arrears. It threatens to cut service to those who owe three months or more.

26 - An agreement is reached after 35 days of meetings in the *concertación* forum, but COSEP doesn't sign. The agreement contains points which: recognize the need to reduce inflation; call for the introduction of the *córdoba oro* as soon as possible at an exchange rate which will promote exports; commit the government to providing the necessary means to bring in the harvest and to rehabilitate small-, medium-, and large-sized industry; agree that the fiscal deficit must be reduced in line with paying attention to social problems; give the highest priority to health and education in the budget and commit the government to not reducing the budget for these areas in 1991; and accept the need to guarantee stability, especially in the next six months.

The Soviet Union and Nicaragua sign an agreement for new economic relations. Nicaragua's debt of $3000 million to the USSR may be renegotiated to be repaid over 40 years. The USSR expressed interest in developing joint ventures in mining.

Reports appear of divisions inside COSEP around the question of whether or not the business group should sign the *concertación* agreements.

Former contras of the Southern Front block the access roads to Yolaina to protest the presence of Sandinista Police and the decision to remove the local chief of the Rural Police.

28 - The FNT says it will propose at the follow-up meetings to the *concertación* agreement that the minimum monthly wage be $240, the cost of a basic shopping basket of 53 products.

A report by the IADB says that Nicaragua was the only country in Central America to show economic improvement in 1989, the last year of the Sandinista administration.

Cardinal Miguel Obando y Bravo comments on the recent *concertación* agreements, saying that they may bring stability but not for long.

29 - General Humberto Ortega meets with more than 25 representatives of the former contras and calls on them to "save the countryside and make demands on the people of the cities and the government."

Some former contras violate the agrarian truce in Region VI and take over some farms (two State-owned and one private) in the Jinotega department.

Reports indicate that former contra leader "Rubén" is stirring up demobilized contras in the town of Las Presillas near Rama. He accuses the government of not complying with the commitments it made. "Rubén" disagrees with "Franklyn's" support of the *concertación* agreement, saying that it legalizes the lands given out by the Sandinistas to themselves while they were in government.

A Liberal leader says that COSEP and Vice-president Virgilio Godoy, with the support of Cardinal Obando y Bravo, are forming a "Vice-presidential movement" to defend Godoy's rights.

30 - COSEP gives a press conference and says it supports the government but thinks that it is ceding too much ground to the Sandinistas. Present at the conference are "Rubén" and contra advisor Aristides Sánchez. "Franklyn" accuses "Rubén" of fomenting instability in the countryside.

The Central American Bank of Economic Integration (BCIE) grants a loan of $20 million, $18 million of which is to repaid within ten years with four years of grace. The money is to be used for a program to promote non-traditional exports.

The Foreign Ministry holds a preliminary meeting with representatives of donor countries to discuss the agenda for a meeting of the Paris Club in early December.

Central Bank President Francisco Mayorga is removed and Dr. Raul Lacayo, one of the bank's Vice-presidents, takes his place.

31 - Lacayo expresses his concern that COSEP appears to be allied with sectors of the contras who are acting against the National Agrarian Commission in its work to find and distribute lands to demobilized members of the Nicaraguan Resistance.

Norway donates $2.3 million for the purchase of transformers in order to rehabilitate the electrical network.

NOVEMBER

1 - COSEP asks that Decree 11-90 (dealing with the privatization of State-owned lands and which is to expire on November 10) be extended.

Former contras take over stretches of the highway to Rama City to demand land and the resignation of General Ortega from the National Agrarian Commission.

6 - Decree 57-90, which extends Decree 11-90, dealing with a review of past property confiscations is issued and will remain in effect until December 31.

7 - From Mexico, Daniel Ortega denounces the existence of a plot to destabilize the government. Groups of armed contras have recently entered the country from Honduras, he says.

After a COSEP assembly, its President Gilberto Cuadra states, "In COSEP, out of principle, we disapprove of anarchy... But we also support fully the demands of the demobilized contras and want a response given—in an orderly fashion without provoking chaos—to those who are demanding the keeping of the promises made in order to have them give up their weapons."

8 - The Episcopal Conference states that "the Church is with the people in making their just demands." The UNO mayors of 18 municipalities do not show up for an appointment with Violeta Chamorro to discuss their demands.

General Ortega says that what is happening is a kind of *coup d'etat* and warns that the laws will be upheld. He also announces that, to date, 5,000 officers have been dismissed from the armed forces as part of the plans to reduce the size of the military. These 5,000 are in "active retirement" and can be called up into the reserves in the event of an emergency. There are now 33,000 members of the armed forces as compared to 96,000 at the beginning of 1990.

9 - U.S. President Bush says that Nicaragua will be included as a beneficiary of the Caribbean Basin Initiative. Nicaragua will be able to export some products to the United States without having to pay import duties.

11 - Cardinal Obando, after mass in the Santa Marta church (his regular church continues to be occupied by protesting members of the Southern Front of former contras) says, "If the problems aren't solved, I think that we could once again get into a war."

14 - U.S. State Department spokesperson Margaret Tutwiler declares U.S. support for President Chamorro and calls for "all segments of Nicaraguan society to work together to strengthen democracy and promote economic reforms."

Finance Minister Pereira announces the 1991 budget to the National Assembly. Of a total of $499 million, 20 percent will be for education, 16 percent for health, and 15 percent for defense. Of a budget deficit of $152 million, Pereira says 91 million will be financed with support from the international community. How the remaining $61 million is to be covered is still unknown.

21 - The International Foundation for the Global Economic Challenge (FIDEG) announces that the monthly inflation rate decreased from 60 percent in September to 30.5 percent in October. Accumulated inflation from January to October is 6,826 percent and the projected figure for the end of the year is 11,000 percent, compared to 1,600 percent in 1989.

22 - "There is hunger in Nicaragua," says Agriculture Minister Roberto Rondon as he presents preliminary plans to reactivate farming and ranching. The average daily intake of calories has fallen from 2,000 to 1,600, and of protein from 54 to 37 grams, while per capita consumption of corn has fallen from 158 to 110 pounds per year and that of beans from 40 to 25 pounds.

24 - In a meeting with General Ortega, Spain's Defense Minister announces a $5 million aid package to help Nicaragua's process of military reduction.

27 - President Chamorro announces the creation of the National Disarmament Commission "to study the problem of unauthorized armed civilians, the manner in which to disarm them, and mechanisms to destroy the weapons thus recovered." At the ceremony, in which 10,000 rifles confiscated since September are buried, Chamorro names former Costa Rican president Oscar Arias honorary President of the commission.

28 - Antonio Lacayo leaves for France and Spain with a government delegation in order to obtain aid so that Nicaragua can renegotiate its $350 million debt to the IADB and the World Bank. Lacayo also mentions that efforts will be made to renegotiate Nicaragua's $240 million debt to Spain. He expresses the hope that $300 million in assistance will be obtained at the meeting of the Paris Club the next week.

Barricada reports the existence of a note from the U.S. AID in which reservations are expressed about the economic plan. Supposedly, the AID has suspended disbursements of the 1990 $300 million aid package and the Central Bank is facing a serious cash flow problem which could provoke a sharp increase in inflation.

29 - Debate on the 1991 budget in the National Assembly remains stagnated. The FSLN bench accuses "extremist" UNO deputies of deliberately blocking approval of the budget until next week in order to sabotage the government mission which is to attend the conference of donor countries in Paris.

The U.S. embassy issues a statement saying that aid disbursements have not been suspended and that $20 million will be coming soon.

30 - An agreement is signed with Canada for the provision of $8.2 million ($9.5 million Canadian) for development projects.

DECEMBER

1 - Vice-minister of Education Belli complains that the 1991 budget allocation for education is too small. He says that primary education will be the hardest hit and that the program of adult education will likely have to be cut. At the same time, education workers are some of the lowest paid public employees.

At a press conference in Madrid, Antonio Lacayo complains about the lack of aid from the United States and says, "The United States could and should do more given that what motivated them to finance the contras for so many years was the necessity for Nicaragua to have a democratic system."

The Health Ministry reports that almost two children die daily in Region VI of diarrhea, measles, bronchial pneumonia, and other illnesses; 403 have died so far this year at an average rate of 13 per week.

4 - The third international conference of donor countries opens in Paris under the auspices of the World Bank. Many countries have been invited to analyze the Nicaraguan economic situation. The Nicaraguan delegation is headed by Antonio Lacayo, and in representation of the FSLN Dr. Sergio Ramírez, Alejandro Martínez, and William Hüpper.
5 - The conference of donors ends with no new commitments for funding being made. A joint World Bank, IMF, and IADB mission is to conduct an on-site examination of Nicaragua's economy in January 1991. The next round of the conference of donors is to be held in March 1991.

This chronology was prepared by María Rosa Renzi and Alejandro Martínez Cuenca consulting the following references:

"Transition and Political Crisis: The Revolution in Nicaragua (1979-86)" by José Luis Coragio and Rosa María Torres (CRIES); "Economic Policy in Nicaragua 1979-88" (CRIES, *Pensamiento Propio*); and a review of Nicaraguan periodicals for the period 1986-90.

Index

About the Author

Dr. Alejandro Martínez Cuenca was born in Managua, Nicaragua on July 22, 1947. He completed his undergraduate studies in Economics and Business Administration at McGill University in Montreal, Canada. He obtained his Master's Degree in Economics at the University of South Carolina and completed his doctoral studies in Macro-economics and Economic Development at Vanderbilt University in the United States. From 1972 to 1978, he was a professor and researcher at the Central American Institute for Business Administration (INCAE) in Managua. He was a consultant for the Interamerican Development Bank (IADB) and the Central American Bank of Economic Integration (BCIE) until February 1979 when he joined the economic team of the FSLN in order to work on the drafting of its economic program. After the revolutionary triumph, he organized the Ministry of Foreign Trade and was the minister from 1979 to 1988. In 1988, he was named as the Minister of Planning and Budget for the Nicaraguan government, a post he held until April 25, 1990. He has founded and heads the International Foundation for the Global Economic Challenge (FIDEG).

About South End Press

South End Press is a nonprofit, collectively-run book publisher with over 175 titles in print. Since our founding in 1977, we have tried to meet the needs of readers who are exploring, or are already committed to, the politics of radical social change.

Our goal is to publish books that encourage critical thinking and constructive action on the key political, cultural, social, economic, and ecological issues shaping life in the United States and in the world. In this way, we hope to give expression to a wide diversity of democratic social movements and to provide an alternative to the products of corporate publishing.

Through the Institute for Social and Cultural Change, South End Press works with other political media projects—*Z Magazine;* Speak Out!, a speakers bureau; the Publishers Support Project; and the New Liberation News Service—to expand access to information and critical analysis. If you would like a free catalog of South End Press books or information about our membership program—which offers two free books and a 40% discount on all titles—please write to us at South End Press, 116 Saint Botolph Street, Boston, MA 02115.

Other titles of interest from South End Press:

Under the Big Stick
Nicaragua and the United States Since 1898
Karl Bermann

Washington's War on Nicaragua
Holly Sklar

Storm Signals
Structural Adjustment and Development Alternatives in the Caribbean
Kathy McAfee

The U.S. Invasion of Panama
Operation JUST CAUSE
Independent Commission of Inquiry on the U.S. Invasion of Panama

Honduras
The Making of a Banana Republic
Alison Acker